DATE DUE

Demco, Inc. 38-293

GOLDEN GATE

GOLDEN GATE

THE LIFE AND TIMES OF AMERICA'S

GREATEST BRIDGE

KEVIN STARR

BLOOMSBURY PRESS

New York • Berlin • London

Published by Bloomsbury Press, New York

All papers used by Bloomsbury Press are natural, recyclable
products made from wood grown in well-managed forests.
The manufacturing processes conform to the environmental
regulations of the country of origin.

LIBRARY OF CONGRESS CATALOGING-IN-PUBLICATION DATA

Starr, Kevin.
Golden Gate : the life and times of America's greatest
bridge / by Kevin Starr.
p.   cm.
Includes bibliographical references and index.
ISBN 978-1-59691-534-3 (alk. paper)
1. Golden Gate Bridge (San Francisco, Calif.)   I. Title.
TG25.S225S74 2010
624.2'30979461—dc22
2009046976

First U.S. edition 2010

3 5 7 9 10 8 6 4 2

Typeset by Westchester Book Group
Printed in the United States of America by Quad/Graphics Fairfield

For my seven grandchildren—
In years to come, may they feel the same thrill as I do
each time the Bridge comes into view.

CONTENTS

-1-

BRIDGE

The Golden Gate Bridge is a global icon, a triumph of engineering, and a work of art. In American terms, it was shaped by the City Beautiful movement, the Progressive Era, and the Great Depression. More mysteriously, the Bridge expresses those forces that science tells us constitute the dynamics of nature itself. Like the Parthenon, the Golden Gate Bridge seems Platonic in its perfection, as if the harmonies and resolutions of creation as understood by mathematics and abstract thought have been effortlessly materialized through engineering design. Although the result of engineering and art, the Golden Gate Bridge seems to be a natural, even an inevitable, entity as well, like the

the final movement of Beethoven's Ninth. In its American context, taken historically, the Bridge aligns itself with the thought of Jonathan Edwards, Ralph Waldo Emerson, and other transcendentalists in presenting an icon of transcendence: a defiance of time pointing to more elusive realities. Were Edwards, Emerson, or the Swedish theologian Emanuel Swedenborg, a mystic thinker of great importance to the formation of American thought, alive today, they would no doubt see in the Golden Gate Bridge a fusion of material and trans-material forces, held in delicate equipoise.

For all that, the Golden Gate Bridge is a bridge. It gets you from one side of the water to the other. Regionally, it serves practical and pragmatic necessity. But here as well iconic forces are at work. Of all American regions, outside Manhattan, California, taken cumulatively, is the most impressive instance of nature rearranged through engineering. From the beginning, water had to be moved from where it was, the north, to where it was needed, elsewhere, as California invented itself through water engineering. The entire Central Valley depended upon irrigation. The port of Los Angeles was blasted by dynamite to sufficient depth. From the Gold Rush onward, most Californians lived in cities and suburbs dependent upon elaborate systems of water and, later, electrical engineering. Yet the early response of Americans in California to the Golden Gate itself was poetic. John Charles Frémont named the entrance to San

Francisco Bay in honor of the Golden Horn of the Bosporus protecting the harbor of ancient Constantinople. William Keith and other American painters in California delighted in depicting it as the entrance to a brave new world of gold and cities to be. A young UC Berkeley philosophy professor by the name of Josiah Royce considered the Gate the perfect symbol of the natural grandeur but philosophical isolation of the remote province in which he found himself.

As early as the frontier era, there were daydreams of spanning the Gate, one of them coming from Joshua Norton, a madman who thought he was an emperor. The early 1920s witnessed the emergence of the grandest daydreamer of them all: Joseph Strauss, bridge-builder, Emersonian visionary, promoter extraordinaire, P. T. Barnum of public works, the Wizard of Oz behind the green curtain. In proposing a bridge, Strauss linked up with an equally emblematic figure, San Francisco city engineer Michael O'Shaughnessy, who was playing a defining role in reconceptualizing and rebuilding San Francisco following its destruction by earthquake and fire in April 1906. As a Progressive, O'Shaughnessy envisioned public works as, among other things, a redemptive enterprise. Public works improved moral tone. In the decades leading up to the construction of the Golden Gate Bridge, Progressives had been busy completing California, rearranging it so as better to serve an emergent society. From this perspective, the Golden

Gate Bridge and its sister structure crossing the Bay to Oakland constituted the last and greatest engineering masterpieces of this post-earthquake Progressive program.

The Bridge, however, had to evolve out of the political process. The Southern Pacific did not want it because it threatened Southern Pacific ferry operations on San Francisco Bay that each workday brought into the Ferry Building at the foot of the Embarcadero some fifty thousand commuters, making it the busiest terminal outside of Charing Cross Station, London. The Navy did not want it. It could be shelled from offshore during wartime and collapse, blocking entrance and egress to the harbor. The environmentalists did not want it. The Bridge seemed an arrogant intrusion on nature. Yet the established governments of the counties ringing San Francisco Bay, together with Del Norte County on the Oregon border, wanted it. Such a bridge would open the Redwood Empire to the north and, more important, further consolidate the counties of the Bay, especially the North Bay counties, with the Bay Area itself, where nearly half the population of California was then living.

A political battle ensued, pitting the Progressive impulse to complete California through public works against other interests and a generalized resistance to change. The Great Depression affected the outcome. Public works provided one of the leading ways Americans were combating unemployment during this era. Yet the Golden Gate Bridge was not a federal project, as was the San Francisco–Oakland Bay Bridge. The Bridge resulted, rather, from a localized, county-driven process; and a private entity, the Bank of America, bought the bonds, bringing into the genesis of the Bridge yet another iconic American, A. P. Giannini, one of the most notable bankers in American history.

Joseph Strauss was a great promoter, but the bridge he initially proposed was a clumsy monstrosity. The Golden Gate could not be defiled with such ugliness. Strauss eventually came to recognize this fact, however reluctantly, and he retained the best bridge designers in the nation to come up with a better solution. The result: engineering as high art, and high art as engineering. And then the color! International Orange, it was called, at once a natural color and a color highly suggestive of artifice, capable of blending into all the hues and colors of the site and the pageant of wind, fog, and maritime weather moving through the channel. Designs complete, bonds sold, supervising engineer Russ Cone and his construction crews got to work. Not since the Brooklyn Bridge was built more than a half century earlier had bridge-builders faced such a challenge. Americans build things, and the construction of the Golden Gate Bridge constitutes an epic achievement of American labor. It is a powerful story—the sinking of the piers, the erection of towers, the spinning and emplacement of cables. Eleven workers lost their lives, ten on one day. Could such a structure be built, one is tempted to ask, without some form of sacrifice? The ancients would have answered *No!* The Golden Gate Bridge represented a defiance of nature as well as a tribute to it, and a certain score had to be settled.

Triumphantly, the Golden Gate Bridge linked the urbanism of San Francisco with the unspoiled headlands of Marin as if to suggest the paradox of California/America itself: a gift of nature, a continent that F. Scott Fitzgerald described as the last place commensurate with the human capacity for wonder, a sacred text, a revelation of the Divine Mind, as far as the Anglo-American Protestant imagination was concerned—yet a place as well to be reshaped into cities, with canals, roadways, railways, highways, aqueducts, bridges, and all those other entities required by urban civilization. Yet the Bridge did not destroy its site; rather, it enhanced it, as the Parthenon enhances the hill upon which it stands. The Golden Gate Bridge announced to the world something important about the American imagination and the American stewardship of the continent, taken at its best. For all their faults, Americans could reform themselves to exercise proper stewardship and would more and more do so, despite the squanderings of the nineteenth century.

From an iconic perspective, the Golden Gate Bridge offers a West Coast counterpart to the Statue of Liberty, announcing, in terms of American Art Deco, American achievement and the higher purposes of American culture. And it does this with its own element of historical narrative, subtly contained in the Art Deco stylization of its towers played off against repetitive cables descending into a reversed arch against an interplay of city, sea, and sky. Lest this all sound too positive, even triumphant, it must be noted that the Golden Gate Bridge, almost immediately, became, literally, the springboard, the platform, for human tragedy, beginning with the great accident of mid-February 1937 that claimed the lives of ten workers. Quite soon, the Bridge became the venue of choice for suicide throughout the greater Bay Area. By 2009 some 1,300 people had ended their lives via the Bridge. What do these seven decades of death by suicide mean? Why have the guardians of the Golden Gate Bridge been reluctant to, as they put it, mar the beauty of the Bridge with suicide-prevention nets or fences? Is this connection of the Bridge to death preventable or inevitable? And if it is inevitable, what does that mean as far as the iconic status of the Bridge is concerned? Here, in any event, where the American continent gives out, the Golden Gate Bridge continues to draw those who have lost what the English novelist Evelyn Waugh has described as the unequal struggle with life.

So hail and farewell, Golden Gate Bridge! You are in the company of the grandest public works achievements of all time; and like these structures, ancient and modern, you serve practical necessity while at the same time encoding meanings multiple and various. Generations have by now been once young and grown old in your company. You have helped to define a culture. You have succeeded in making nature even more beautiful through engineering and art. In times past, you were constructed, foot by foot, cable by cable, bolt by bolt. But you also descended as golden Fire from abstract Number in a manifestation that the ancients would have understood. Like Rockefeller Center, you continue to celebrate the best capacities of Art Deco. Your color remains a joyous fusion of nature and artifice. You were built to last for a thousand years, and both your permanence and your vulnerability testify to your greatness. Do you foretell a better world, ordered as you are ordered, according to utility and grace? Or will human beings, ages from now, gaze upon your ruins and marvel at the American nation that once bestrode the continent and the resourceful citizens of that once great but now lost Republic?

-2-

ICON

According to Eastern Orthodox Christianity, an icon, the Greek word for image, is more than a symbol. While a symbol can signify or point to something larger, an icon embodies the forces that are being signified. Thus from an Orthodox Christian perspective, an icon is not only an image of the sacred, it is itself a sacred object. Most world religions nurture something akin to this belief. With their theologized Puritan heritage, Americans shared this sense of the iconic; indeed, for the great eighteenth-century theologian Jonathan Edwards, briefly president of Princeton University, the American continent itself was a sacred text to be read, simultaneously, as a natural and a sacred event. When he presented us with the Great White Whale of *Moby-Dick* (1851), Herman Melville did more than present us with a symbol. The whale, Captain Ahab fails to understand, with tragic consequences, was not only a sign of the sacred innocence and otherness of nature, it was also a living manifestation of this truth, intensified to transcendental proportions.

Nor were Americans oblivious to the iconic power of engineering and architecture. Hence the taste for classicism in the decades of the early Republic, as Americans sought to link their society with what they believed to be the democratic republics of the ancient world. Hence the taste for Gothic Revival as romanticism swept the nation in the early mid-nineteenth century, with its suggestions of older and more picturesque cultures. And hence the triumph of steel and glass industrialism, in factories and train stations initially, but carrying over into skyscrapers as well, despite a tendency to design these new structures with some sense of historical reference. But so too, when it came to engineering, did Americans behold in each new turnpike, lighthouse, canal, aqueduct, or reservoir proof positive of an assured destiny for the American Republic.

When it came to such symbology, a bridge was easy to understand. Within the classical context, so beloved by the early Republic, the bridge, as structure and symbol, had been enshrined in Roman religion and the state in the title Pontifex Maximus, the great bridgemaker, given the high priest of the ancient Roman College of Pontiffs. Bridges led from one place to another, hence signified the passage to and from one world to another through religion, which underlies the social compact. In time, the Roman emperor assumed this title, Pontifex Maximus, as a matter of course, and in the mid-fourth century of the Common Era it passed over to the Bishop of Rome, the Supreme Pontiff or Pope.

Bridges connected the sacred and profane. Bridges suggested journeys between time and eternity. Bridges also branded cities with signature landmarks. Medieval Florence is ineluctably linked to the Ponte Vecchio (1345), which extended the city across the Arno in a stone-built promenade of shops and residences. London Bridge (1831) was not only built and rebuilt across the years, destroyed by fire after fire and falling down in a well-known nursery rhyme, it was upstaged in 1894 by the Tower Bridge, a marvel of steel construction and steel-based technology masked in a neo-Gothic sheath, announcing, like the buildings of Parliament, that here, in this city, London, one quarter of the planet was ruled in an empire upon which the sun never set. When a new city in that empire, Sydney, wished to express its coming of age as an urban entity, along with the coming of age of the new nation it served, it also built a bridge, the Sydney Harbour Bridge (1932), the widest long-span bridge in the world, which in time would frame the Sydney Opera House (1974), both structures becoming leading icons of a new world city.

For a generation of post–World War I writers and intellectuals living and working in New York, the Brooklyn Bridge (1883) did more than signify the triumph of post–Civil War industrial technology. The Bridge embodied the hope that the subsequent industrial era did not, of necessity, have to result in a dehumanizing civilization. In its beauty and civil urbanism, the Brooklyn Bridge—its piers sunk deep into the East River, its neo-Gothic towers rising against the Manhattan skyline, its service through its pedestrian culture of the city as theater and human community—embodied a better nation to come or, at the least, offered writers and artists seeking such a better nation the personal comfort that such a finer America might be achieved.

Thus Italian-born artist John Stella portrayed the Brooklyn Bridge in 1919 as a futurist rendering of the brave new world to which he had immigrated; and thus Lewis Mumford, an aspiring literary, architectural, and cultural critic, experienced through the Brooklyn Bridge the transforming notion that modern construction did not have to be ugly and oppressive. The Brooklyn Bridge led Mumford to explore, throughout the 1920s, the literary and architectural history of the nation in search of usable patterns for future development: the search for a usable past, as Mumford's friend

Van Wyck Brooks understood it, launching himself as well into a lifetime search for patterns in American culture, as revealed through literature, that might inspire a developing American society. And thus Hart Crane, a young midwesterner of Anglo-American descent, also spent a good part of the 1920s—the decade in which the Golden Gate Bridge was being designed and prepared for construction—employing the Brooklyn Bridge as the imaginative matrix for a notable American poem.

Written in response to T. S. Eliot's *The Waste Land* (1922), descrying the emptiness of modern civilization, Crane's *The Bridge* (1930) at once offers tribute to Eliot's modernity of poetic technique while at the same time rejecting Eliot's dismissal of modernity as a moral and psychological dead end. Encountering the Brooklyn Bridge by dawn, walking across it by night, en route to the towers of Manhattan in the distance, Crane experiences the bridge as a triumph of engineering offering a portal into the American past—from Columbus to the conquistadores, from Pocahontas to Rip Van Winkle, from the Gold Rush to the settlement of the Midwest, from the construction of the transcontinental railroad to the invention of the airplane, from the rise of industrialism to the creation of New York City and the construction of the Brooklyn Bridge itself—and offering as well, finally, the hope that modernity, meaning industrialism and the machine era, can be made to serve productive purposes.

Guiding Crane on his imaginative journey, like Virgil guiding Dante in the *Pugatorio*, is the affirming presence of Walt Whitman, the great yea-sayer of nineteenth-century America. Challenging Whitman's optimism is his contemporary Edgar Allan Poe, poet and short story writer of trauma, doubt, and despair. Much too brief to be considered an epic, Crane's seven-part poem is nevertheless epic in its intent, seeking to subsume unto itself, via the mystic alchemy of the Brooklyn Bridge, the totality of American experience. Modernism has destroyed much in its wake, the poet admits, and there remains the possibility of even further destruction and loss. Yet the cables curving gracefully downward from their neo-Gothic towers to support a roadway between river and sky suggest also that the age of engineering and the machine, subways, skyscrapers, and airplanes, may also be productive of good. Even more, the bridge may offer an experience of time and transcendence. The cosmos itself reverberates through the orphic strings of the bridge's supporting cables, creating one song, one bridge of fire, linked to the stars themselves and to the deepest human desires for Cathay, meaning for Hart Crane perfection of place, fulfillment in the social order.

Elliptical and elusive, modeled on the vatic Ur-poem of the twentieth century, fully cognizant of the perils and terrors of modern life, Hart Crane's *The Bridge* nevertheless ends on a note of hope. Its historicism, however oblique, fits into the search for a usable past characteristic of an entire generation of New York City writers. For Crane, the Brooklyn Bridge is not merely a symbol of the American history he is construing. It is, rather, its living embodiment, its icon, offering not only knowledge and interpretation but the actual experience of human culture, art and engineering, the American past, and, indeed, the cosmos itself, things seen and unseen yet known through imaginative and spiritual experience.

The American Society of Civil Engineers ranks the Golden Gate Bridge as one of the Seven Wonders of the Modern World, along with such other choices as the Channel Tunnel, the Empire State Building, and the Panama Canal. As such, the Golden Gate Bridge is in its eighth decade of interpretation since 1937. Ever since ancient times, when the Greek historian Herodotus and the poet-scholar Callimachus of the Library of Alexandria first drew up lists of the Seven Wonders of the Ancient World, the great architecture and engineering marvels of human creativity have been interpreted not only for how they are designed and what needs they serve, but for what they mean as well in the larger scheme of things. In the United States such icons of engineering and design ingenuity have included, among others, the Erie Canal, the Panama Canal, the Empire State Building, and the Hoover Dam, each of them relatively easy to decipher in their social and cultural significance. Serving the ambitions of an expanding nation, the Erie Canal (1825) linked the Hudson River with the Great Lakes and thereby established these vast inland bodies of water as deep-sea ports, empowering the emergence of a second rim of cities and population after the East Coast. Serving the needs of an emergent imperial Republic, the Panama Canal (1914) linked the Atlantic and the Pacific oceans and thereby fostered trade and established the United States as a two-ocean naval power. The Empire State Building (1931) capped a decade that had witnessed the emergence of New York as the paradigmatic American city. The Hoover Dam (1936) organized the water and hydroelectrical resources of the arid and semi-arid West, thereby empowering the cities of the region to grow into population centers.

Like the Brooklyn Bridge, the Golden Gate Bridge bespeaks the triumph of modern engineering and technology on a global scale, but also with special relevance to California, a region that had to be reassembled through engineering and technology before it could reach its potential. Like the Brooklyn Bridge as well, the Golden Gate Bridge facilitated and accelerated the rising urbanism of the area it served. Like the Hoover Dam, the Golden Gate Bridge assured an American generation that the Great Depression that was causing such suffering could, finally, be surmounted through an interaction of public and private investment. And like all such engineering and architectural wonders, of whatever place or clime—be they the Great Pyramid of Giza, the Great Wall of China, Hagia Sophia, Chichen Itza, or the Taj Mahal—the Golden Gate Bridge to this day makes a statement regarding the interaction among material culture and social purpose and the elusive mysteries of human aspiration and achievement within the context of time and transcendence.

- 3 -

SITE

The Golden Gate Bridge serves as the focal point and organizing principle of a fusion of nature and history that is at once a matter of geography and public art. In the perceptions of those encountering it, the Bridge and its site reflect eons of geological time and a shorter period of human association. As drama, then, the Bridge celebrates that interaction of nature, technology, and social purpose that created Native American, Spanish, Mexican, American, and ultimately global California across centuries of human development.

It took more than one hundred million years for Planet Earth to achieve this stunning composition of land and water at longitude 122 degrees, 31 minutes west and latitude 37 degrees, 48 minutes north on the Pacific Coast of the North American continent. As the great rivers of Northern and Central California formed themselves in the interior in ages past, they began over time to converge into a unified sixteen-river system, itself the product of thousands of tributary streams, that poured into a great valley and moved westward to the sea, bringing along uncountable amounts of sand, gravel, and mud, which coalesced into stone and sediment formations on the valley floor. The weight of this sediment cracked the earth's crust, and over the eons a ring of mountains was thrown up around the rim of the valley. As the flow of water into the valley converged even further, it cut a great gorge, the Strait of Carquinez, into the valley basin and began to push against the mountain barrier that had been thrust up on the western edge. Eventually, some several hundred thousand years ago, the river created a cleft in the barrier and transformed the alluvial plain to the west into a great marshland. This marshy plain extended westward to as far as the present-day Farallones.

When the climate began to warm some 200,000 years ago, and the great glaciers of the north began to melt into the sea, the ocean rose and covered the marshland and began to push back against the fresh waters pouring westward through the cleft. Some 125,000 years ago, the force of the rising ocean overcame the force of the flowing waters from the interior. The cleft was widened and deepened, and the waters of the ocean flowed into the valley floor, creating a great inland bay. Then came another ice age, and the waters of the ocean receded. The bay became, once again, a valley, and the strait into the bay became, once again, a marsh-land extending westward. Then it happened all over again. Around 27,000 years ago, the ice once more began to melt, and the ocean again rose and its waters again pre-vailed against the river, moving east to west, flowing into the valley floor.

This second great watering of the bay floor took thou-sands of years and might have been under way as recently as a few thousand years ago, which perhaps accounts for its story making its way into Native American lore. For human beings were now present, for thousands of years, on the floor of the marshy valley. As that bay rose, these people—Coast Miwok to the north, Wappo and Lake Miwok to the north-east, Miwok to the west, and Costanoan (Ohlone) to the south—learned to live on the 100 miles of shore lining some 450 square miles of water formed by four conjoined bays creating one vast inland sea. In time, great mounds of seashells, calcified into natural formations, would testify to the feasting by generations of these peoples of the shores of the great bay now formed. Of all the Native American peoples living in California during these centu-ries, these people can be said to have enjoyed the easiest of lives, the fattest of deer and elk, the greatest abundance of shellfish.

During the last years that Native Americans would be able to enjoy their ancient way of life, Spain, having established itself in Mexico and Baja California, was exploring northward up along the coast. This era of reconnaissance lasted for more than two hundred years and involved a veering west across the Pacific to the Philippines. But the maritime expeditions of Spain failed to discover the entrance to the great bay. The Cabrillo expedition sailed past it in 1542. Returning from Asia in 1565, the Cermeño expedition, wrecked at Point Reyes, sailed past it in a reconstructed launch, and in the time to come, the yearly Manila galleon continued to sail past the entrance. The English missed it in 1579 when Francis Drake anchored his *Golden Hinde* in Drake's Bay north of the channel. In search of a harbor where Manila galleons might find shelter after their harrowing voyage across the Pacific, the Vizcaíno expedition of 1602–3 sailed past the Golden Gate and, failing to discover the bay within, exaggerated the suitability of Monterey Bay to the south so as not to have the expedition seem a failure. The Golden Gate was narrow, for one thing, approximately a mile wide, and it stood at the end of a long strait that acted as a funnel and stabilizer for fog. If a ship were passing on the far side of the Farallon Islands, thirty miles offshore, seeing the Gate would be impossible. The bay off the California coast remained undiscovered as far as Spain was concerned, from 1542 to 1769, which is to say, for the 227 years that Spain was active—at least once a year in the form of the Manila galleon. For as many as twenty-five generations or more, then, the Native Americans living around the great bay enjoyed it in tranquillity, kept safe by the dense fogs concealing its narrow opening.

Today, the Golden Gate Bridge is caressed by the same fogs that obscured the Gate for centuries. The same river of fresh water, draining the same 40 percent of the land mass of the interior, still rushes westward through the Gate, at the rate of more than half a million cubic feet per second in winter months, a greater flow than that of the Colorado River; and the same Pacific still, twice a day, pours its 2.3 million cubic feet of saltwater per second through the channel; and for the same twenty minutes, twice in a twenty-four-hour cycle, the strait remains calm in the same way. Overhead, the same prevailing westerlies continue to blow at speeds ranging from twenty to sixty miles per hour; and under the surface of the water, the same fish, seals, and sea lions continue to swim in and out of the Gate that nourishes them, and the same crabs crawl along the sea floor. The oyster beds, alas, which fed generations of Native Americans and flourished into the early twentieth century—when a young Jack London earned money as an oyster pirate, harvesting on behalf of the restaurants of San Francisco—are long gone. Each of the natural features of the bay the First Californians knew—the points and headlands, the ten islands, the shores, hillsides, and mountains in view—still maintain, some of them, their Native American designations. Most of them, however, now bear Spanish and English names, testifying to the historical development that ensued and would leave its mark.

In October 1769 the seasoned Spanish soldier Gaspar de Portolá, the first Spanish governor of the Californias, picked his way with a contingent of soldiers up the mountainous coast north of Monterey Bay. After more than two centuries of inactivity, Spain had at long last mounted a Sacred Expedition to Alta California for purposes of exploration, evangelization, and settlement. As military commander of the expedition, Portolá wanted to know what lay north of Monterey Bay, which he failed to connect with the bay described by Vizcaíno 166 years earlier, so exaggerated was Vizcaíno's assessment. Could it be that the great bay described by Vizcaíno lay farther to the north? Portolá asked himself, pushing on, accompanied by the learned Friar Juan Crespi. Arriving at Half Moon Bay, Portolá recognized certain landforms described by Vizcaíno—the Farallones, Point Reyes, and Drake's Bay. On Tuesday, October 31, 1769, the Portolá expedition encamped in the coastal range in the vicinity of Half Moon Bay, and Portolá sent Sergeant José Francisco Ortega out with a search party of eight men. While Ortega and his men were gone, on November 2, some other soldiers, out hunting deer, climbed the hills northeast of their camp and returned with the exciting news that from the summit they beheld a great inland sea stretching north, south, and east as far as the eye could see.

The Ortega party had made the same discovery the previous day and was conducting a reconnaissance of the southern shore. On November 10, Sergeant Ortega and his men returned to camp and rejoined the main party. Comparing reports, the Spaniards realized that they had come upon a bay that Father Crespi described as so large that "doubtless not only all the navies of our Catholic Monarch, but those of all Europe, might lie within the harbor." Having run out of supplies and feeling more than a little lost, the Portolá party returned southward to Monterey.

Three years later, in March 1772, Captain Comandante Don Pedro Fages, also accompanied by Father Crespi, set out north from Monterey to reconfirm what the Portolá expedition had seen in 1769. This time, the Fages expedition conducted a reconnaissance of the eastern shore of the Bay, from which, somewhere in the vicinity of the present-day city of Oakland, climbing into the hills, they looked across the Bay, east to west, and beheld the Golden Gate on Thursday, March 26, 1772, which they named La Bocana de la Ensenada de Los Farallones, the Mouth of the Bay of the Cliffs. The next day, moving farther north to the site of the future campus of the University of California at Berkeley, they climbed the slopes of Grizzly Peak, looked down through the straits, and beheld the Farallones. Skirting the south shore of San Pablo Bay and the Delta Country, they beheld the great Central Valley and, in the distance, could see the snow-capped crests of the Sierra Nevada.

On this second visit, Father Crespi recorded in his diary for March 27 a reconnaissance and mapping of the strait leading into the mouth of the Bay, through which the Spaniards could see three islands—Angel, Alcatraz, and Yerba Buena. Two years after Fages and Crespi had stood atop Grizzly Peak in the East Bay and looked across the water to the headlands, Captain Fernando Rivera y Moncada, now the military commandante of Alta California, led yet another exploring party north from Monterey, this time proceeding up Ocean Beach on the western edge of the San Francisco peninsula. The Spaniards climbed Point Lobos, overlooking the strait and entrance to the Bay. Through this strait, following his pilot, José de Cañizares, by a day, Juan Manuel de Ayala sailed the *San Carlos* on August 6, 1775, fighting a strong current and a westerly wind that made him fear for the safety of his sails. Anchoring, finally, in a calm off the shoreline of what would later be known as the city of Sausalito, the *San Carlos* had become the first ship to sail into San Francisco Bay.

To look through the Golden Gate Strait today, east to west, is to experience the visual evidence of the subsequent history that—slowly at first, then picking up momentum in the 1830s and 1840s, and exploding into the fast-forward of the Gold Rush in 1849—followed this early reconnaissance by Spain. To the north are the Marin Headlands, preserved in their pristine condition as part of the Golden Gate National Recreation Area. Today, the headlands are no longer darkened by vast herds of tule elk, as they were in times past, although small numbers of surviving elk do graze contentedly on the federally protected slopes to the north. Through the Bridge, just to the south, are equally rolling headlands on the northern edge of San Francisco. These hills, however, are densely planted in pine, cypress, and eucalyptus and offer a display, even from offshore, of military buildings; for in the summer of 1776 they were established as a presidio to guard this northernmost reach of New Spain.

Lieutenant Colonel Juan Bautista de Anza first camped here with his men in late March 1776, on the shores of Mountain Lake, partially filled in 161 years later to create a foundation for Doyle Drive leading to the Golden Gate Bridge. On September 17, 1776, after de Anza had returned to Mexico, his second in command, Lieutenant José Moraga, raised the standard of King Carlos III of Spain and founded a presidio on flatlands northeast of Mountain Lake. That October Franciscan missionaries dedicated a mission inland on a grassy slope near a small lake, which they called Laguna de los Dolores, the Lake of Sorrows, in honor of the Seven Sorrows of the Blessed Virgin Mary. The mission was named San Francisco de Asís, in honor of the founder of the order, but the name of the nearby lake prevailed, and it became known as Mission Dolores. The name San Francisco, however, was formally attached to the village of Yerba Buena, Mexican since 1822, when it was organized as an American city on January 30, 1847. While Mission Dolores is too far inland to be seen from the Bay, the American city that can be traced back to the presidio and mission established by the Spanish in 1776 now unfolds on the southern shoreline, rising on its many hills like Atlantis from the sea, by turns shrouded in fog—a cool gray city of love, its poet laureate George Sterling called it—or in neo-Mediterranean color when the afternoon sun has burned off the fog, as it does nine months a year, and bathes the city in golden light.

Hundreds of abandoned sailing ships were crowding the harbor by late 1849 when a great Gold Rush brought thousands to California from around the globe and propelled the newly established American city into what historian H. H. Bancroft later termed a "rapid monstrous maturity." In his *Geographical Memoir* (1848), John Charles Frémont, assisted by his wife and co-author Jessie Benton Frémont, described how he in 1846 had named and mapped the entrance to San

Francisco Bay as Chrysopylae, Greek for Golden Gate, in honor of the Chrysoceras, or Golden Horn, delineating the harbor of ancient Byzantium refounded as Constantinople in 330 of the Common Era. The form of the Byzantine harbor suggested a golden horn, Frémont argued, while at the same time evoking the riches of commerce that would pass through its strait. So too would the name Chrysopylae, the Golden Gate, foretell the commerce that would one day pour through this Pacific strait and the city such commerce would create. A mere three years later, Frémont's prediction came true, as during the first full year of the Gold Rush (1849) hundreds of ships sailed through the strait and into San Francisco Bay, and a ramshackle overnight city, not yet a Constantinople but heading in the right direction, grew up on a cove at the northern edge of the San Francisco peninsula.

A maritime colony, served directly by tall-masted, sail-crowded clipper ships laden with cargo for the city and the mines of the Mother Lode, and by great side-wheeler steamers, some of them capable of carrying up to a thousand passengers, San Francisco was urban from its beginning, bypassing completely the slow, patient development of an agricultural frontier. This destined urbanism, so obvious today in the beautiful city alongside the Bay south of the Golden Gate, has even further corroboration in the assertive urbanism observed from Bay or Bridge alike. Slightly to the southeast cluster the high-rises of the downtown, and beyond these rise the four towers of the San Francisco—Oakland Bay Bridge, passing through Yerba Buena Island, which first caught the attention of Spaniards so long ago. On the eastern shore is the white sweep of Oakland and Berkeley, where the great campanile of the University of California rises against the green backdrop of the Berkeley hills, atop which the Spaniards looked to the west and saw the entrance to the Bay and looked to the east and saw, across a great valley, the Range of Light, the Sierra Nevada, in the far, far distance.

Cities encapsulate time, and so all this resplendent urbanism expresses the enterprise and development of the American era. The *San Carlos* and the clipper ship *Flying Cloud* and the side-wheeler *Golden Gate* have yielded to freighters and tankers, passenger cruise ships, and military vessels, passing under the Bridge in either direction on any given day, or the white flecks of sailing craft replacing the lateen sails of the feluccas in which Italian fishermen once ventured forth from San Francisco in the late nineteenth century. To the north of the Bridge, on the southern shores of Marin, the bayside communities of Sausalito, Belvedere Island, and Point Tiburon remain hidden from view until well past the Bridge and into the Bay, yet offshore from the Marina district of San Francisco they dramatically assert themselves: Sausalito, in whose cove New England whaling ships, up from the South

Pacific, anchored for food, water, and refurbishment in the 1820s; Belvedere, where in the 1880s and 1890s San Franciscans found refuge from summer fogs, building there New England–style seaside homes; and Point Tiburon, where the railroad serving the northern counties began and terminated in times past, and where a Riviera-like suburban enclave emerged in the post–World War II era.

In the Bay itself, the three islands first seen by the Spaniards in the 1770s now reverberate with successive phases of previous history. On Angel Island the Immigration Service for years ran the central receiving station for what little immigration was allowed from Asia. On the walls of the cell-like rooms in a surviving structure can be deciphered Chinese characters expressing the anxieties, the outright fear, the despair even, of interned Chinese awaiting, for so long, legal or medical clearance. Atop Alcatraz Island, named by the Spaniards for the pelicans that alighted there, still sits the ominous federal prison that in 1933 replaced an earlier military detention barracks. What a paradox! To have in the midst of such a setting, redolent of natural beauty and human achievement, such an ominous structure. For more than thirty years, until the prison was closed in 1963, long-term and lifetime detainees—whose numbers included such iconic figures as Al Capone and Machine Gun Kelly—could hear as they lay in their cells dance music and laughter wafting across the water from the St. Francis Yacht

Club. In the distance, Yerba Buena Island receives the first section of the San Francisco–Oakland Bay Bridge via a tunnel running through it, and on the waters below, also visible from the Golden Gate Bridge, extends the flat surface of the man-made Treasure Island created atop shallow shoals as the site for the Golden Gate International Exposition of 1939, which celebrated the completion of the San Francisco–Oakland Bay and Golden Gate bridges. Acquired by the Navy in April 1941, Treasure Island has once again become a neighborhood of San Francisco.

Here it is, then, framed by the Golden Gate and its Bridge, the *plenum mundi*, the fullness of the world: Bay, ships, cities, island, other bridges, great universities, hills and headlands everywhere, all of it vibrant with present-tense energy and rich associations from a storied past. Here is the epicenter of the fourth-largest metropolitan region in the nation, and certainly one of the most compelling in its dramatic interplay of natural beauty and an equally attractive built environment. In terms of geological time, the human achievement everywhere so evident constitutes less than a nanosecond in duration; and even when measured in terms of historical time—from the moment Spanish explorers first beheld the great Bay from a high point on the Coast Range—the time-lapse of it all barely exceeds two and a half centuries. Yet despite the brevity of human engagement, how much has been achieved in so short a time, reflecting the rapid rise of the American Republic itself, which shares with the Bay Area the year 1776 as a foundational date. Spain that year established a presidio and a mission loyal to the crown, while on the other shore of the continent the Founding Fathers declared their independence from another king. In time the two jurisdictions would come closer to each other when Mexico broke from the Spanish crown and declared itself a republic. In 1846 the two orders fused when American ships of the line sailed into San Francisco Bay and a detachment of naval personnel raised the Stars and Stripes over the Mexican village of Yerba Buena, soon to be renamed San Francisco.

-4-

VISION

Roads, railroads, ferry boats, and automotive highways helped bring the Golden Gate Bridge into existence. But before the Bridge could be built, it had to be envisioned. Imagining the Bridge began as early as the 1850s and reached a crisis point by the 1920s. In this pre-design and pre-construction drama of vision, planning, and public and private organization, four figures played important roles. Marin County businessman James Wilkins and San Francisco city engineer Michael O'Shaughnessy first called for the Bridge to be built, engineering entrepreneur Joseph Strauss agreed to do it, and banker Frank Doyle, president of the Santa Rosa Chamber of Commerce in Sonoma County, played a crucial role in persuading the counties north of San Francisco that a bridge across the Golden Gate would be in their best interest. Dreamers and doers, each of these men helped initiate a process that would after a decade of negotiation enlist hundreds of engineers, politicians, bankers, steelmakers, and, of equal importance to all of them, construction workers, in a successful effort to span the strait with a gently rising arc of suspended steel.

First came the roads, or, more correct, the one great road: El Camino Real. The Golden Gate Bridge facilitates a linkage established by Franciscan missionaries in the late eighteenth century. Moving north from the first mission, San Diego de Alcalá, El Camino Real—the Royal Highway, the King's Highway—linked the twenty-one missions founded between 1769 and 1823 at intervals of a day's march. A traveler moving from Mission Dolores on the San Francisco peninsula, however, to Missions San Rafael Arcángel and San Francisco Solano in the North Bay would be forced either to circumnavigate the Bay from the east or to be ferried across. After 1937, the Golden Gate Bridge provided a direct access to these two missions. Thus, for all its modernity, the Golden Gate Bridge completed the vision of Spanish Franciscan missionaries of an Alta California unified by one Royal Highway along the coast from San Diego to the North Bay.

To this day, El Camino Real remains part of a state highway system underlain by coastal Native American trails, which formed the basis not only of El Camino Real but of numerous cattle trails in the Spanish and Mexican eras. These cattle trails, in turn, frequently morphed into toll roads in the American frontier era, railroad connections in the late nineteenth century, streetcar lines in the fin de siècle, and unpaved and paved roadways in the first years of the twentieth century. In 1912 the first highway to be paved by the newly established California Highway Commission was an historic stretch of El Camino Real in Burlingame, San Mateo County. In each instance, vision initiated the process, beginning with the vision of the Franciscans of coastal California as a string of missions, or the vision of Spanish army officers of coastal California as a network of presidios, or the vision of Spanish and Mexican rancheros of coastal California unfolding as a linkage of land grant ranchos.

All things considered, the railroad came early to California. As early as 1854 work began on a railroad connection, the first in the state, between Sacramento and the town of Folsom twenty miles distant. By 1860 a steam engine of local manufacture was linking San Francisco and San Jose in the South Bay. As early as December 1854, in a speech before the Mechanics Institute in San Francisco, Dr. Oliver Wozencraft was calling for a railroad linking California with the rest of the continent. In 1857 the Rensselaer

Polytechnic—educated engineer Theodore Judah, who had supervised the construction of the railroad between Sacramento and Folsom, outlined in a pamphlet the exact route such a trans-Sierran railroad might take via Dutch Flat, Donner Lake, and Lake Tahoe.

An expanding rail and roadway system required numerous bridges. The crossing of the Sierra Nevada in the mid-1860s involved the construction by Chinese workers of railroad trestles of unprecedented magnitude; and, in the decades that followed, as it expanded its intra-California network, the Central Pacific (Southern Pacific after 1885) maintained a bridge-building bureau that embellished California with a network not only of wooden trestles but of impressive bridges of gray granite that to this day remain valued legacies of nineteenth-century engineering. Calls to bridge San Francisco Bay came with equal rapidity, as early as 1851, in fact, when William Walker, editor of the *San Francisco Herald*, called for an extension of the two-thousand-foot Clay Street wharf as a causeway to Oakland that would rest on wooden piers in the shallows and pontoons of anchored barges in deep water. Two years later San Francisco physician D. G. Robinson built and exhibited a model of a bridge across the Bay. In February 1853 State Senator W. H. McCoun rose in chambers to introduce a bill granting railway and wagon rights of way to anyone successfully bridging the Bay. A popular song of the day, meanwhile,

In 1869 Joshua Norton, the self-styled Emperor of the United States and Protector of Mexico, called for the construction of a bridge from Oakland to Yerba Buena Island and from thence to Sausalito. *(Courtesy of the Bancroft Library, University of California, Berkeley)*

"The Song of the Oakland Bridge," lyrics by Charles Mackay, music by Stephen Massett, urged San Franciscans to build such a facility. Perhaps the best-known of all these early calls for a bridge across the Bay came on August 18,

1869, from the delusional San Francisco eccentric Joshua Norton, the self-styled Emperor of the United States and Protector of Mexico, a failed commodities speculator supported by handouts as part of local color. However delusional he might have been in his imperial status, Norton I in retrospect seems visionary in calling for the construction of a bridge from Oakland to Yerba Buena Island and from thence to Sausalito. His Imperial Majesty betrayed his true state of mind, however, when he called for the bridge to continue west until it reached the Farallones.

By the 1870s the Central Pacific knew that it had a problem. Its transcontinental railroad maintained its central roundhouse and repair facility in Sacramento. North of San Francisco Bay, one line turned east into the Central Valley. The other serviced San Francisco and its hinterlands from the eastern inland side of the Bay. That involved connections by ferry boat for those arriving in or departing from San Francisco or a separate train ride up from San Jose. Thus came the calls, quite early, for the bridging of San Francisco Bay via a railroad trestle and the construction of a grand terminal on the waterfront, where the transcontinental railroad would arrive and depart. In 1871 a panel of engineers recommended the construction of a combination causeway and two drawspans from Mission Bay in San Francisco to Oakland, facilitating railroad, horsecar, wagon, carriage, and pedestrian traffic and of sufficient width to allow for housing and retail development. San Francisco supervisor Charles R. Story went so far as to submit a resolution to the board calling for a special election to issue construction bonds, a move that Story's fellow supervisors opposed, given the twelve-year free pass for use of the structure by the Central Pacific that Story had written into the legislation. As part of the debate, the notion of a causeway was replaced with that of a suspension bridge in the anonymous pamphlet *The Railroad System of California* (1871); yet the suspension bridge proposal—however more safe and efficient than the causeway model—was not sufficient to boost the San Francisco Bay Bridge proposal beyond a mere matter of speculation, given the general opposition to affording the Central Pacific free passage across the Bay. Finally, in 1906, the Southern Pacific built its own trestle across the shallows of the South Bay between Dumbarton Point and Palo Alto.

The Southern Pacific and a few other companies, meanwhile, got into the ferry business, and by the mid-1920s, on a working weekday, some fifty thousand commuters moved in and out of San Francisco by ferry. The Ferry Building itself, on the Embarcadero at Market—before which phalanxes of streetcars brought ferry commuters to their final destination—became the busiest terminal of its kind in the nation. As far as weekday commuter culture was concerned, this era of ferries on San Francisco Bay seems

in retrospect a kind of golden age. In the East Bay, the interurban trains and streetcars of the Key System brought commuters swiftly and safely to the Oakland Mole and other
points of embarkation. Once aboard the commodious ferries, commuters enjoyed a scenic trip of no more than thirty
minutes. Carrying hundreds of passengers, cities afloat, the
ferries offered a full range of eating, newsstand, or shoe-
shine services. Growing attached to one another, commuters played bridge or poker or used the time to read a
newspaper or prepare for the day's work. Ferry service to
Berkeley, connecting so easily to the city's extensive streetcar system, helped keep Cal a commuter university for San
Francisco through the 1920s and 1930s.

The problem was the automobile, especially on weekends and especially when it came to the Marin–San Francisco connection. Residents of Oakland, Hayward, Berkeley,
and the other communities of the East Bay tended to take
their recreation in the larger East Bay itself. San Franciscans, however, and residents of the peninsula to the south
had long since developed a preference for Marin and Sonoma counties for weekend trips and summer vacations.
The Russian River area in Sonoma abounded in resorts,
community-based encampments, and privately owned summer cabins, reachable by narrow-gauge railroad or, later,
via automobile on the Redwood Highway. Marin County,

meanwhile, still significantly undeveloped, offered numerous opportunities for hiking, camping, visits to the redwoods, and beach life, as well as extended summer sojourns. As the age of the automobile gained momentum, it took more and more time for ferries to embark or disembark automobiles heading into the North Bay from the Embarcadero in San Francisco or Sausalito in Marin. Late afternoons and early evenings on Sundays were especially troublesome, when weekenders returning to the city could expect to wait in their automobiles one, two, even three hours for ferry transport back to San Francisco.

One San Franciscan for whom this delay was especially galling was city engineer Michael O'Shaughnessy; and from O'Shaughnessy came the most influential early suggestion for bridging the Golden Gate. O'Shaughnessy embodied and activated the civic forces behind the rebuilding of San Francisco following the earthquake and fire of April 1906. Starting in the 1890s, San Francisco—queen of the Golden West, financial and social capital of the Pacific Coast—had begun to take itself seriously as far as architecture and planning were concerned. Throughout the decade and into the twentieth century, a generation of notable architects—a number of them graduates of the École des Beaux-Arts in Paris, some of them veterans of leading New York firms, others self-taught in a profession that still allowed entrance

Circa 1902 photograph by R. J. Water and Co. shows the expanse of the Golden Gate on a sunny day. Prior to the building of the Bridge, ferry boats carried commuters across the Golden Gate, with as many as fifty thousand passengers leaving or arriving in San Francisco on a busy week-day in the mid-1920s. *(Library of Congress)*

through practical training—were busy designing and constructing for San Francisco public and private buildings appropriate to the status of the city as a regional capital and a center of Asia/Pacific trade and commerce. When the earthquake struck early on the morning of April 18, 1906, much of this newly achieved urban fabric—public buildings, including the city hall, hotels, office towers, schools, clubs, and private residences—was either lost or severely damaged. Just prior to the earthquake, the famed city planner Daniel Hudson Burnham of Chicago, commissioned by the Association for the Adornment and Beautification of San Francisco, had submitted to the board of supervisors a plan calling for the improvement of San Francisco along the City Beautiful lines Burnham had helped implement in Chicago and Manila. With San Francisco in ruins, Burnham rushed back from Paris in the belief that his plan would be immediately enacted.

Instead, faced with the necessity of rebuilding as quickly as possible, San Franciscans rebuilt their city in three short years on the basis of its 1847 grid. Still, the dream of San Francisco rising from its ashes as a City Beautiful—a grand composition of plazas, boulevards, parks, and public spaces—did not go away. It remained in the minds of the controlling oligarchy of the city as a continuing premise for political and planning reform. Thus when self-made shipping magnate James Rolph, a bipartisan Progressive Republican, was elected in 1911 to the first of five terms as mayor, he saw as one of his most important challenges the retrofitting and upgrade of San Francisco, in many instances according to recommendations first made in the Burnham Plan. To supervise such an ambitious program, Rolph needed a city engineer of undisputed ability, and so he turned to Michael Maurice O'Shaughnessy.

Born in County Limerick, Ireland, in 1864 and taking his degree in civil engineering from the Royal University of Dublin twenty years later, O'Shaughnessy in 1885 immigrated to San Francisco, one of the most Irish cities in the nation, and prospered there as a surveyor for the Southern Pacific. He married a local girl, then opened his own engineering office in 1889. From the beginning, O'Shaughnessy was connected to public projects: laying out the towns of Mill Valley and Sausalito in Marin, serving as chief engineer for the California Midwinter International Exposition of 1894 in Golden Gate Park, working on commissions for the privately owned Spring Valley Water Company that supplied the city. Broadening his practice, O'Shaughnessy moved to Hawaii, where he supervised the construction of several major water projects, then left Hawaii for San Diego, where he was enjoying a lucrative practice of some $30,000 per year as a dam and water engineering consultant when Mayor Rolph invited him for an interview on the last day of August 1912 in the Hotel Whitcomb, then serving as the temporary city hall.

It was a momentous interview. O'Shaughnessy, for one thing, was still resentful of San Francisco's reluctance to pay fees owed him as a consulting engineer, which had motivated his move to Hawaii. Employing his formidable gifts of persuasion, Mayor Rolph laid out for O'Shaughnessy a dazzling prospect, the continuing improvement of a notable American city recovering from catastrophe. There was the

Hetch Hetchy project, first of all: dam, aqueduct, reservoir, and distribution system bringing the waters of the Tuolumne to San Francisco and its hinterlands. Once the city purchased the Spring Valley Water Company, O'Shaughnessy would run the entire system. A great new city hall was in the planning stages, scheduled to open in 1915, the same year as the Panama-Pacific International Exposition celebrating the recovering of the city. O'Shaughnessy would be in charge of the design and construction of the infrastructure for the 1915 fair. Streetcar tunnels needed to be dug and put into operation beneath Twin Peaks and Parnassus Heights, opening the southern and western portions of the city for development, together with an automotive tunnel on Stockton Street in the downtown, to unify the city in a north-south direction. A new high-pressure water system was needed to prevent a recurrence of its failure during the earthquake. The Burnham Plan had called for a Great Highway along Ocean Beach on the western edge of the city, and that too would be built under the supervision of the city engineer, along with dozens of other roadway projects. He would be in charge of all this, Rolph told O'Shaughnessy, and he would be free from political interference. Urged by his homesick wife to let bygones be bygones and accept the mayor's offer, O'Shaughnessy took a 50 percent pay cut and accepted the position of city engineer of San Francisco.

Thus the most compelling imperatives of the Burnham Plan now came under the jurisdiction of, all things considered, one of the most powerful city engineers in the nation. While not included in Rolph's program, the challenges of designing and building a bridge to Oakland and a bridge to Marin across the Golden Gate were at the least implicit in it. Each of these entities would be necessary for the fulfillment of San Francisco's grand dream of rebuilding itself, better than ever, as the epicenter of an emergent Bay Area, a regional capital in the Far West, and a center of trade and commerce, scheduled, after the completion of the Panama Canal in 1914, to be linked simultaneously to Atlantic and Pacific trade. For San Francisco to achieve in the most complete manner possible its civic and commercial destiny, it had to be joined more completely to its hinterlands.

The Panama-Pacific International Exposition of 1915 brought to San Francisco an engineering entrepreneur and inventor, Joseph Baermann Strauss of Chicago, destined to promote into being a global icon of bridge engineering and design. Born in Cincinnati in 1870 of German Jewish ancestry, Strauss had studied engineering at the University of Cincinnati and qualified as a civil engineer. Engineering, specifically the building of bridges, galvanized and focused Strauss's multiple ambitions. There was something dreamy, mystical even, in Strauss, an intensity of poetic feeling that led him to a lifelong composition of poetry and a poetic desire to do something grand and great with his life. Strauss resisted the role of Jew as outsider, preferring instead to be in the thick of things. At the University of Cincinnati, he brought Sigma Alpha Epsilon to campus, the second national fraternity to arrive. Five foot three and slender in physique, he tried out for the football team and was sent to the university infirmary to recover from injuries.

While in the infirmary, Strauss enjoyed a clear view of the Cincinnati-Covington Bridge. Designed by the great John August Roebling in the mid-1840s and completed in 1867, the Cincinnati-Covington Bridge was the first long-span suspension bridge—more than a thousand feet across the Ohio River into Kentucky—to be built in the United States. As he recovered from his football injuries, Strauss had time aplenty to enjoy his view of the bridge and, in that mysterious alchemy of conscious and subconscious forces so characteristic of developing young people, to have the bridge take hold of his mind as a poetic engineering statement uniting beauty and practical achievement. Chosen to speak at his graduation, Strauss read from his senior thesis proposing a bridge across the Bering Strait.

It would take nearly forty years for Joseph Strauss to have a comparable project in hand, a bridge across the Golden Gate. In the meanwhile, Strauss entered the world of bridge engineering following his graduation in 1892. Joining the New Jersey Steel and Iron Company of Trenton, Strauss spent the decade 1892–1902 as a draftsman, inspector, detailer, and estimator of railway bridges and viaducts in New Jersey and, later, Chicago, where in 1902 he established his own firm. Strauss's specialty was the bascule, or counterbalanced, drawbridge, allowing for the tilting upward of a bridge segment through the employment of cast-iron counterweights. A lifelong inventor by instinct, always seeking a better way to do things, Strauss improved bascule technology, patented his design, and made his Strauss Bascule Bridge Company of Chicago a leader in its field, responsible for more than four hundred bascule bridges across the nation.

It was bascule technology and the Panama-Pacific International Exposition of 1915 that first brought Strauss to San Francisco. His firm designed and built the Aeroscope, an enclosed viewing platform atop a bascule steel arm capable of lifting up to 120 sightseers 260 feet above the Joy Zone of the Exposition for a stunning view of the fair, San Francisco, the Bay, and the hills of Marin. It was the most popular ride at the Exposition, and it led to a contract from city engineer O'Shaughnessy for the Strauss company to provide the superstructure for a bascule bridge across Fourth Street south of Market that to this day remains in use.

On Sundays, Michael O'Shaughnessy, who knew Marin

County very well from his early experiences there surveying and laying out Mill Valley and Sausalito, was accustomed to take the ferry to Sausalito and ramble through the hills and forests around Mill Valley. On these rambles, O'Shaughnessy became increasingly aware of just how suitable for suburban development was southern Marin, centered on Mount Tamalpais. But first the Golden Gate Strait had to be bridged. Increasingly delayed at the ferry embarkation point in Sausalito on his return to the city, O'Shaughnessy grew more and more intrigued by the prospect of a bridge across the Golden Gate.

There is a strong possibility that O'Shaughnessy either derived his notion of a bridge to Marin or was reconfirmed in it by a series of articles in August 1916 in the *San Francisco Bulletin* by Marin engineer James Wilkins, calling for the construction of a $10 million suspension bridge between Lime and Fort points, the two closest points on the San Francisco and Marin shores respectively. The comprehensive range of Wilkins's articles inserted him into the company of Golden Gate Bridge founders, for they constituted the most complete and persuasive proposals to that date. In addition to these articles, Wilkins personally briefed O'Shaughnessy on his proposal and won the approval of the San Rafael City Council, the Central Marin Chamber of Commerce, and the Marin Board of Supervisors. This support, coming so rapidly in the late summer of 1916—and no doubt mentioned by O'Shaughnessy in his conversations with Strauss—most likely helped to convince both men that the Golden Gate Bridge project was politically feasible.

Still, there was a world war in progress, in which California and the nation were involved, as well as a closely fought presidential contest, in which California would make possible the victory of Democrat Woodrow Wilson over Republican Charles Evans Hughes. The Golden Gate Bridge proposal faded from the headlines but not from the drawing boards of the Strauss Bascule Bridge Company at 225 North Michigan Avenue in Chicago, where designs for the bridge were being developed at Strauss's expense. Early on in the process, O'Shaughnessy had realized that the design of such a bridge was beyond his expertise. He was a civil engineer, with expertise in the design and construction of water projects—dams, aqueducts, reservoirs—with a secondary expertise in sewers, waterlines, tunnels, and roadways. The design and construction of bridges was another matter entirely. O'Shaughnessy also realized that even if he had the expertise, the financial requirements for such a bridge would more than likely be beyond the ability of San Francisco and rural Marin County. Still, as city engineer, he was the man responsible for the upgrading, indeed the completion, of San Francisco, and a

bridge across the Golden Gate, however remote in its possibilities, was of necessity part of that larger pattern of
development.

O'Shaughnessy got into the habit of discussing the possibilities of such a bridge with the bridge-builders he encountered. He was approaching them, most likely, as
possible consultants or subcontractors, to work under his
direction, should the city and county of San Francisco or
the state of California or the federal government or a kind
of public/private joint entity not yet thought of undertake
the Golden Gate Bridge project. At some point during the
Panama-Pacific International Exposition or the construction of the Fourth Street Bridge, O'Shaughnessy added
Joseph Strauss of Chicago to the roll call of bridge-builders
with whom he was conferring regarding the bridging of
the Golden Gate.

What O'Shaughnessy was not prepared for, most likely,
was the conversion, swift and overwhelming, of Joseph
Strauss to the project. Here for the Chicago-based entrepreneur was not just another bascule bridge, of which he had
built hundreds. Here was a challenge requiring an accomplishment comparable to John Roebling's with the
Cincinnati-Covington Bridge and the great Brooklyn Bridge
itself: an opportunity for a bridge designer to go down in
history alongside the greatest bridge-builders of modern

times. By 1921 Strauss and O'Shaughnessy, acting as joint sponsors of the project, were in a position to announce their proposal in a fifteen-page prospectus, replete with illustrations and statistics: a bridge across the Golden Gate, 6,700 feet or 1.6 miles in length, a mixed-type design consisting of two fixed-frame cantilevered structures resting on concrete piers north and south joined at the center via a suspension span. The brochure designated O'Shaughnessy and Strauss as sponsors, with Strauss taking responsibility for the brochure itself—and certainly for the glowing terms introducing the Bridge. "The project of a bridge across the Golden Gate," Strauss wrote, "hithertofore considered a wild flight of the imagination has, through recent advances in engineering and bridge design, become a practical proposition. It is a project that appeals, for aside from its commercial and financial attractiveness and its great practical value, it will represent a crowning achievement of American endeavor and will constitute the greatest structure in point of magnitude and span ever erected. In such a product of the Great Golden West, America could build a peace memorial that would fitly commemorate the close of the World War and the dawn of the Age of Republics."

In the decade following the war that Strauss wanted the Bridge to commemorate, ferry-borne automobile traffic across San Francisco Bay was in the process of increasing

Chief engineer Joseph B. Strauss, captured on the construction site by *Life* magazine photographer Peter Stackpole. *(Courtesy of the Bancroft Library, University of California, Berkeley)*

seven-fold, moving toward three thousand automobiles on a single holiday weekend. The fleet was capable of handling, at maximum, no more than a thousand cars an hour. Since most of the three thousand commuters to the north preferred to return to San Francisco around sunset after a full day, this could translate to a delay of up to three hours in Sausalito as they waited in line to embark. Providing dress rehearsals for the two main events, the Golden Gate and the San Francisco–Oakland Bay bridges, the American Toll Bridge Company started construction in April 1923 of a cantilever bridge across Carquinez Strait between Contra Costa and Solano counties, which opened in 1927. In January 1926 the American Toll Bridge Company completed a two-lane vertical-lift span bridge across the mouth of the San Joaquin River in the Delta between the city of Antioch and Sherman Island, linking Sacramento and Contra Costa counties. A year later, a privately sponsored truss-lifted span bridge opened between Newark and Menlo Park in the South Bay, followed in March 1929 by another private bridge, a causeway with drawspan joining San Mateo and Hayward. As late as 1930, the Bay Cities Bridge Corporation, a spin-off of the American Toll Bridge Company, was proposing a rail and highway causeway between Alameda Island and the Santa Fe and Southern Pacific railyards on Sixteenth Street in San Francisco. The growing automobile traffic of the 1920s, in short, was bridging the Bay and Delta with private sector structures. These examples might in time have led to private bridges between San Francisco and Oakland and across the Golden Gate, had there not been a Great Depression. As it turned out, the state of

California, financed by a Reconstruction Finance Corporation loan from the federal government, would construct the San Francisco–Oakland Bay Bridge, and a new kind of entity, a county-based bridge and highway district, would finance and build the Golden Gate.

-5-

POLITICS

For either the San Francisco–Oakland Bay Bridge or the Golden Gate Bridge to be built required political will. At this point, the political sponsorship of the two projects diverged. The San Francisco–Oakland Bay Bridge came under the aegis of state government: the legislature, the governor, the Division of Highways, and the Toll Bridge Authority. The Bay Bridge also attracted the attention, and ultimately the crucial sponsorship when he became president, of Herbert Hoover of Palo Alto, then serving as secretary of commerce in the administrations of Warren Harding and Calvin Coolidge. A mining engineer by training, Hoover had in the course of his career sponsored construction projects in Australia and China. Gathering a team of Stanford classmates around him during the First World War, Hoover had organized the Committee for the Relief of Belgium, saving that war-torn nation from starvation. Following the armistice, he performed similar services for Germany, Poland, and Russia. As secretary of commerce, Hoover played an important role in the development of the national highway system, the organization and administration of radio airwaves, and the developing field of air traffic control. He negotiated the Colorado River Compact resulting in the construction of Boulder Dam, later renamed in his honor. Herbert Hoover was, in short, a skilled engineer, a highly placed public servant, a devoted alumnus of Stanford, where he served as trustee, and a loyal citizen of the Bay Area. As president, he would authorize a $72 million loan from the Reconstruction Finance Corporation for construction of the San Francisco–Oakland Bay Bridge, to be repaid from toll revenues. The Golden Gate Bridge, by contrast, had neither state nor federal sponsorship, although the state of California, after intense debate, did authorize a freestanding bridge and highway district, and the War Department, fearing threats to military navigation, with reluctance approved both bridges. The Golden Gate Bridge required local support, which is to say, the immediate support of local politicians, local bankers, and the business and agricultural communities.

Following the publication of the brochure *Bridging "the Golden Gate"* in 1921, Joseph Strauss, while maintaining control of his engineering firm in Chicago, charged with the full force of his Napoleonic personality into the role of chief spokesman for the proposed Bridge. While remaining an important advocate of the Bridge, city engineer O'Shaughnessy, now in the full tide of numerous construction projects, yielded this role to Strauss, who was spending more and more time in the Bay Area, speaking on behalf of the project. Slight of voice, tending to get lost in technicalities and statistics, Strauss nevertheless proved a compelling platform presenter, given the messianic fervor emanating from his diminutive but dapper presence as he gave countless talks in the Bay Area and the North Bay counties promoting the Golden Gate Bridge to whatever group would listen.

Enter Frank Doyle, president of the Exchange Bank, the largest financial institution in Santa Rosa, and president as well of the Santa Rosa Chamber of Commerce. Frank Doyle was a local man, a Santa Rosa, Sonoma County man, respected and influential. Born in Petaluma in 1863 and educated in local public schools and Heald's Business College in San Francisco, Doyle had risen quickly in the Petaluma Water Company, becoming manager in 1886. Four years later, Doyle helped his father found the Exchange Bank of Santa Rosa, where he served as cashier until 1916, before becoming president. Dapper, with a taste for good tailoring, his mustache and beard neatly trimmed, Doyle brought a note of urbanity to the North Bay, where in addition to his duties at the Exchange Bank he served as a director of two banks in nearby Sebastopol and a local water and power company, as well as a Santa Rosa–based mortgage company. As treasurer of the Redwood Highway Association and president of the Santa Rosa Chamber of Commerce—as well as a leading figure in the Odd Fellows, Elks, Rotarians, and Native Sons of the Golden West—Doyle functioned as the grand bourgeois of his city and region. No public venture was complete—or successful—without his presence.

In person and through press reports, Doyle heard Strauss's message loud and clear, and it reverberated with Doyle's own sense of what was needed. For the North Bay—Sonoma, Napa, Lake, and Mendocino counties—to develop into more than a sparsely settled agricultural and ranching region, it would have to have a more immediate contact to San Francisco than the ferry system currently allowed. In 1911 Jack London had described the counties north of San Francisco as the Switzerland of North America and predicted their rise as a state and national tourist destination. London, however, had toured the region in a horse-drawn wagon. By the 1920s, the tourist trade had gone automotive and required a highway connection to the population centers of San Francisco, the peninsula, and the East Bay.

By the end of 1922, thanks to Strauss's tireless campaigning, the Golden Gate Bridge project had gained wide support from the boards of supervisors of San Francisco and Marin, newspapers, civic groups, and booster clubs of every sort. By December 1922 there was talk—much of it coming from the office of Mayor James Rolph, prompted by city engineer Michael O'Shaughnessy—of a regional meeting to promote the project. Which is exactly what Frank Doyle and the Santa Rosa Chamber of Commerce organized in mid-January 1923. Impressively, more than three hundred delegates from twenty-one Bay Area and Northern California counties convened in Santa Rosa on January 13, 1923, for a two-day meeting. Mayor Rolph was on hand, as was O'Shaughnessy, along with a large delegation of San Francisco supervisors, Napa assemblyman Frank Coombs, assorted politicians, bankers, newspapermen, and even the president of the Golden Gate Ferry Company, who was telling one and all that there would be enough business for everybody. Only Joseph Strauss—back in Chicago, minding the store—was missing. Frank Doyle chaired the meeting and was eloquent in his support of the proposal, as were dozens of other speakers. In the course of the two-day meeting, two important votes were taken: to form a Bridging the Golden Gate Association and to draft legislation for a new kind of public entity, a multi-county Golden Gate Bridge and Highway District, which Assemblyman Coombs could sponsor in Sacramento.

Following the Santa Rosa meeting formally launching the Golden Gate Bridge project, there ensued a decade of political struggle over organization and finance that at times threatened to put the Bridge indefinitely on hold. Given the Great Depression of the 1930s, followed by the Second World War, such a delay might have lasted into the post-war period. As it was, this saga of politics and courtroom battles delayed by five years Strauss's promise to begin construction by 1927. And yet, once the battle was over, supporters of the Bridge had doubly, triply gained the right to design and build what was, to that point in time, the most ambitious bridge of its kind in human history. Superheated fires forged the steel of the Golden Gate Bridge. Superheated politics forged the consensus necessary for its design and construction. The dynamics of this struggle revolved around a few key questions. Was the Bridge, first of all, truly necessary? Was it safe? Should the public or private sector, or a combination thereof, pay for it? If the Bridge were to be built, what kind of organization would build it? And who would be in charge? Given the outcome of these questions, a suspension bridge across the Golden Gate, a decade of political struggle, while exhausting, closely fought, and almost derailing, was nevertheless worth the effort and, in the long run, necessary.

As pro-Bridge forces returned to their home bases in mid-January 1923, their first requirement was to achieve the passage of a state-authorized bridge and highway district. All things considered, this first phase of organization went smoothly. For some three decades and more now, for one thing, thanks to the Wright Act of 1887, the state of California had been authorizing multi-county irrigation districts empowered to issue bonds, raise money, construct irrigation projects, and administer ongoing irrigation programs. To create such a state-authorized entity for a bridge project, then, did not require any new theory, only the extension of an existing practice. Nevertheless—once Assemblyman Frank Coombs of Napa introduced in the assembly in February 1923 a Bridge and Highway District Act—the Bridging the Golden Gate Association, taking no chances, organized a full-court lobbying effort, with Strauss as chief spokesman. In contemporary parlance, Strauss stayed on message. In 1922 alone, he pointed out, more than 300,000 automobiles, out of a total Bay traffic of 1.8 million automobiles, had crossed the Golden Gate by ferry. Indeed, in that very year, the creation of a second ferry company, Golden Gate Ferry, had entered the market to supplement the crowded ferries of the Northwestern Pacific Railroad, a subsidiary of Southern Pacific. According to the Motor Car Dealers Association of San Francisco, a watery Great Wall of China was in the process of sealing off the city.

Next to no opposition surfaced in the short month in which the bill was heard and passed in May 1923. Indeed, legislators went out of their way to pass a joint resolution requesting that the War Department approve the project, as required by law. It took approximately a year for Strauss and his team of volunteers from the Bridging the Golden Gate Association to submit renderings and statistics to the War Department in Washington. On May 16, 1924, Colonel Herbert Deakyne, district engineer for the Army Corps of Engineers, presided over a hearing in San Francisco City Hall. The key issue, as far as the Corps of Engineers was concerned, Colonel Deakyne pointed out, was the danger that a bridge across the Golden Gate might obstruct shipping in peacetime and, if destroyed in war, block San Francisco Bay. Then there was the question of earthquake, a sensitive point for a region shaken to its foundations in April 1906. The dreaded San Andreas Fault passed a mere 5.6 miles to the east.

In their testimony, Strauss and O'Shaughnessy countered these objections. As far as peacetime traffic was concerned, the Bridge would be well lit, hence provide improved guidance for ships entering or leaving the Bay. In case of an offshore bombardment in time of war, the channel was deep enough between piers to absorb a fallen structure without obstructing shipping. And as far as earthquakes were concerned, that was a danger faced at all times by the entire Bay Area, and the proposed Bridge would be made as earthquake resistant as possible through advanced engineering design. Newspapers reported no serious counter-testimony during the three-hour meeting, and a poker-faced Colonel Deakyne closed the meeting with an announcement that he would send his recommendation to the War Department. Eight months later, in a letter dated December 20, 1924, Secretary of War John Wingate Weeks gave his approval and authorized the Bridging the Golden Gate Association to continue with its plans.

Next up: the organization of the Bridge District. There was only one serious delay. Given the preponderance of San Francisco's population, argued the San Francisco Board of Supervisors, San Francisco should have at least half of the directors on the board of the Bridge District. The North Bay counties agreed, and the legislature quickly passed an amendment. San Francisco also wanted assurance that any bonds issued by the District would not affect the bonding limit of San Francisco. That too was agreed upon, and in April 1925 San Francisco joined the District. By November Marin, Sonoma, Napa, Mendocino, and Del Norte had also joined, while Humboldt and Lake counties declined membership. A sparsely settled coastal county on the Oregon border, Del Norte County saw the proposed Bridge as an opportunity to end its isolation. Lake County, by contrast, felt itself too poor to enter the program, and in Humboldt the lumber interests that controlled the county saw the Bridge as a threat to their continuing influence. As long as

Humboldt County remained isolated and sparsely settled, the lumber companies ran the show. Develop Humboldt County, they believed, and their influence would wane.

At this point, with all the paperwork filed in Sacramento with Secretary of State Frank Jordan, serious trouble surfaced. Swayed by ranching and lumber interests, the board of supervisors of Mendocino County repealed its ordinance joining the District. The very existence of the District now stood in peril. Taking to the offensive, the officials of the Bridging the Golden Gate Association filed a lawsuit in the name of its president, Frank Doyle of Santa Rosa. In *Doyle v. Jordan*, the association argued that the change of ordinance by Mendocino County was illegal and that Secretary of State Jordan should proceed with the incorporation of the Bridge District. In August 1926, the California State Supreme Court upheld the validity of the Bridge Act of 1923 as amended in 1925. The ordinance of intention filed by the Mendocino board of supervisors, the court determined, could not be rescinded.

As *Doyle v. Jordan* wound its way through the courts, numerous amici curiae protests were filed—902 from Mendocino, 823 from Napa, 574 from Sonoma, fewer than 10 each from Marin and San Francisco, and none from Del Norte—from landowners arguing that they were being deprived of their property without due process of law through taxes being levied without their approval. The court rejected this argument, but nevertheless called for hearings, to be conducted by Judge C. J. Luttrell of Siskiyou County, in which some 2,308 property owners would have an opportunity to express their desire to be excluded from the Bridge District. Not only did these hearings, held in San Francisco and throughout the counties concerned, offer dissenting taxpayers a chance to be heard, they also opened the door for attacks on Strauss's design for the Bridge and on Strauss personally. The Taxpayers' Protective League submitted a hostile review of the Strauss proposal from the Joint Council of Engineering Societies of San Francisco, written by two consulting engineers and Charles Wing, chair of civil engineering at Stanford. The consulting engineers, J. B. Pope and W. J. H. Fogelstrom, and Professor Wing went so far as to testify personally before Judge Luttrell that U.S. Coast and Geodetic Survey reports proved that the rock formations under the proposed south pier could not withstand the load and that Strauss's estimation of the cost, $27 million, was far too low. A bridge across the Golden Gate, they argued, would actually cost more than $112 million, and that in turn meant that property owners would not only have to pay tolls to cross the Bridge but would also be assessed for approximately $120 million over a forty-year period before the bonds could be retired. As if all this were not enough, Pope, Fogelstrom, and Wing—establishment engineers all, with strong local reputations—suggested that Strauss was an under-qualified outsider from Chicago, in town to drum up business.

Although Strauss flew out from Chicago in November and refuted these claims before Judge Luttrell, serious damage had been done to the reputation of the project. It took until November 1928, moreover, a year after Strauss had initially promised he could finish the Bridge, for Judge Luttrell to hear all 2,300 cases and hand down his ruling. Disallowing all protests from San Francisco, Marin, and Sonoma counties, Luttrell nevertheless allowed some property owners in Napa and even more in Mendocino to withdraw from the District. On December 4, 1928, Secretary of State Jordan issued a certificate of incorporation establishing the Golden Gate Bridge and Highway District, which took only six weeks to organize itself, hire staff, and establish headquarters in San Francisco City Hall.

With Strauss under such personal attack, the directors conducted a nationwide search for district engineer and interviewed a number of highly qualified candidates before appointing Strauss, who by that time had earned the sometimes begrudging respect of all directors and stakeholders. The directors nevertheless did not confer on Strauss undivided authority but established instead a board of engineers reporting directly to the District. Over the next three years, Strauss's design would be scrapped entirely, and Strauss himself, coming under stress, would absent himself from the project for a half year. Yet Strauss had managed to survive serious damage to his reputation and serious questioning of the geological foundations of the project. Strauss continued to do that which, from the beginning, he had done so well: inspire in others a belief that the straits of the Golden Gate should and could be spanned.

Provided it could be paid for. An initial levy of taxes enabled the District to finance the redesign of the Bridge from Strauss's Chicago headquarters. Indeed, the Golden Gate Bridge project was soon Strauss's only client. Construction costs, however, were another matter. Millions of dollars would be needed. That meant the issuance of bonds to be repaid with interest from Bridge tolls, and for such bonds to be sold to private syndicates, all doubts regarding the feasibility of the Bridge had to be dispelled. Almost immediately following his appointment, Strauss retained the services of Professor Andrew Lawson of the University of California as consulting geologist to oversee a resurvey of the rock formations beneath the proposed site for the south pier of the Bridge. Not only was Lawson a nationally respected geologist, he was also an expert on the San Andreas Fault and related earthquake issues. With Lawson's guidance, a Minneapolis firm began sixteen diamond-drill borings on the sites of all proposed anchorages and piers.

Since the Bridge was substantially redesigned by April 1930, the War Department announced that it wanted to review its approval of 1924. Only the intervention of California senators Hiram Johnson and Samuel Shortridge persuaded the War Department to rescind its call for a new review. In the interim, however, critics of the Bridge went on the attack, publicly and through private channels, and the War Department reversed its reversal and called for a public hearing. Fortunately, the War Department stated that it was only interested in the matter of Bridge clearances and not the geological suitability of the site, standing by its approval of 1924. Sensing an opening, the Pacific American Steamship Association and the Shipowners' Association of the Pacific Coast retained the blue chip San Francisco law firm of Brobeck, Phleger & Harrison to draw up a twenty-two-page brief declaring the Bridge a danger to shipping and submitted it to the board of officers appointed by the chief engineer of the U.S. Army to review the case.

For all its elaborate argumentation, the anti-Bridge brief came down to a matter of thirty feet of vertical clearance. Two hundred fifty feet, the lawyers argued, and not the proposed 220 would be necessary to handle shipping traffic over the next fifty years, given the increasing tonnage of freight and passenger ships. As it was, eight existing vessels would have trouble clearing the proposed Bridge. Not so! countered the pro-Bridge experts. Current building trends favored a lower, sleeker profile for ship design over the high-masted designs of the past. And besides: the 220-foot clearance figure was not a constant. It was only an absolute minimum. Clearance beneath the Bridge increased at low tide, and the Bridge itself would contract under various weather conditions. In August 1930 Secretary of War Patrick Hurley issued a ruling in favor of the Bridge. It could proceed to construction according to the plans submitted to the War Department in April.

Warming up for a $35 million bond issue, the Golden Gate Bridge and Highway District published in late August 1930 a three-volume report covering all phases of bridge engineering, traffic management, and social and economic benefits. Supervised by Strauss, the three-volume report represented a bold counterattack on all arguments against the Bridge, especially those made by the Joint Council of Engineering Societies in 1927–28. With the George Washington Bridge, under construction since 1927, serving as a model for comparison, an outside board of New York–based engineers reaffirmed a $32,815,000 cost for the span. And as far as structural and aesthetic issues were concerned, Strauss's 1921 design had been scrapped, and the

Bridge redesigned completely, as evident in volume three of the report. This three-volume justification constituted the most coherent raison d'être and manifesto to date; and as such, given the fact that all public works must make the transition from vision to proposal to articulated justification, this report, for which Strauss served as demiurge and executive producer, must be seen as the controlling document for the Golden Gate Bridge and hence ranks as one of the most important engineering reports, in terms of its outcome, in the history of American construction.

A good thing, too, for the report had to withstand two more years of hostile scrutiny from Bridge opponents. To the usual arguments—the Bridge was too costly, tolls would prove insufficient to redeem taxpayer-backed bonds, the geological foundations for the south pier were inadequate—the Sierra Club added an environmental objection, relatively uncommon at the time. The Bridge, the Sierra Club argued, would profane its site. The venerable San Francisco writer Gertrude Atherton concurred, and so did many upper-crust San Franciscans of a certain vintage, who had come to maturity and grown old in sight of the strait, and at least one young San Franciscan, aspiring photographer Ansel Adams, who had grown up in the Sea Cliff district alongside the strait and could not imagine its grandeur surviving the construction of the world's largest suspension bridge. Adams, however, sensing that the Bridge would be built, made a series of elegant photographs of the empty Gate, capturing an immemorial grandeur that would soon be not marred but enhanced by the most beautiful bridge ever built.

-6-

MONEY

Aesthetics, however, even aesthetics based in environmentalism, would not prove the decisive factor. Money was the issue. First, voters in the Bridge District had to be persuaded to approve a $35 million bond issue in the aftermath of the stock market collapse of October 1929 and the still-uncertain efforts of the Hoover administration to deal with the ensuing crisis. Raising a $50,000 war chest from non-tax sources and organizing a speakers' bureau with a full-time director, the Bridge District launched a campaign of speeches, radio spots, and newspaper advertisements organized around two compelling themes, one oriented toward the Bay Area, the other toward the North Bay.

As far as San Francisco was concerned, where the majority of the voters lived, the Golden Gate Bridge and the San Francisco–Oakland Bay Bridge were equally necessary to end the geographical isolation that had kept San Francisco bottled up on its 46.38-square-mile peninsula, while Los Angeles, since 1920 the largest city in the state, was expanding across its uninterrupted plain en route to commanding metropolitan status. And as far as the North Bay was concerned, together with Del Norte County on the Oregon border, there could be little significant social and economic development in these regions, including tourism, without improved automotive and trucking access to the Bay Area. If the economies of the Bay Area and the North Bay were being currently challenged, it could only grow worse for both the Bay Area, if cut off from its hinterlands, as well as for the hinterlands, if sealed off from their energizing metropolis.

As might be expected, the opposition went into overdrive. Shipowners repeated their requirement that the vertical clearance be raised to 250 feet. Even more threatening, the shippers took their lobby directly to the president, the secretary of war, the mayor of San Francisco, and to a host of other local, state, and federal officials. A newly organized Taxpayers' Committee Against the Golden Gate Bridge Bonds launched a radio and newspaper ad campaign emphasizing the precariousness of the American economy. The

Taxpayers' Committee also reheated and rehearsed the 1927 anti-pier site arguments of the Joint Council of Engineering Societies. Comprised in significant measure of established San Franciscans, the Commonwealth Club of California passed a resolution that it was an inopportune time to obligate taxpayers for bond issues that bridge tolls might not be able to redeem. Unkindest cut of all, especially as far as Joseph Strauss was concerned, city engineer Michael O'Shaughnessy, beset by cost overruns at his Hetch Hetchy project, also came out against constructing the Golden Gate Bridge at this time: this from the man who, along with Strauss, jointly issued the initiating Bridge proposal of 1921!

Despite this opposition, the District won the November 1930 election with a margin of better than three to one, eight to one in Marin and Sonoma counties, thanks, in part, to the enlightened self-interest of such organizations as the California State Automobile Association, the San Francisco Motor Car Dealers, the Redwood Empire Association, and Marvelous Marin, promoting better automotive access between San Francisco and the North Bay. On Labor Day weekend 1930, their arguments were doubly, triply reinforced as more than eighty-six thousand vehicles brought the ferry system to a near standstill. Automobiles heading for the ferry slip in Sausalito were backed up for fifteen miles, with congestion not cleared until well past midnight.

Defeated at the polls, the Southern Pacific and Golden Gate ferry companies took to the courts and launched a three-year saga of legal maneuvering that prevented, as it turned out, both the sale of the bonds that had been authorized by the voters and the possibility of federal loans from the Reconstruction Finance Corporation. If all this were not enough, bond consultants on the East Coast were demanding that, prior to the first offering of $6 million in bonds scheduled for July 1931, the District itself go to court to precipitate a legal ruling that would clear away any lingering doubts regarding the bond issue. The directors refused, believing that a state statute validating each and every step taken by the Bridge District in issuing the bonds would suffice. The state passed such a statute in March 1931; but when bids opened in July, only one offer was made, and this from a San Francisco house stating that, given the weakening bond market, it also would require a ruling from the California State Supreme Court that the bonds were legal and, as far as the court could determine, a good faith investment, backed legally by taxpayers in the District and redeemable from bridge tolls.

At this point, a second possible investor, a syndicate headed by Bankamerica Company of California, expressed interest in the $6 million offering, but with the same requisite: a court case clearing away all doubts. Thus the District had no choice but to force litigation by having its secretary, W. W. Felt Jr., refuse to endorse the bonds over to the Bankamerica syndicate and thereby allow the District to sue its own secretary. *Golden Gate Bridge and Highway District v. Felt* wended its way through the courts during the following year, which allowed the anti-Bridge coalition to resurface—yet again!—with all of its anti-Bridge arguments and for the ferry companies and other assorted opponents to file amici curiae briefs opposing either the bond issue or the project in its totality.

The good news was that the Bridge District eventually prevailed in the federal district court. The bad news was that the anti-Bridge lobby had been given the opportunity for a third cycle of attack. Public opinion, however, was mounting against the ferry companies, especially the Southern Pacific. The San Francisco Board of Supervisors went so far as to threaten to demand that the Southern Pacific substantially improve its Hyde Street terminal or vacate the city-owned property. A new mayor, Angelo Rossi, mediated an interim agreement, but the Southern Pacific refused to rule out the possibility that it would fight the bond issue all the way up to the U.S. Supreme Court, tying up the project for years to come.

The Bankamerica syndicate, meanwhile, was asking slightly more than the 5 percent interest authorized by the voters, and this forced the District to investigate the possibility of a loan from the Reconstruction Finance

Corporation (RFC) in Washington, even to contemplate making the Bridge a project of the California Toll Bridge Authority, as was the case with the San Francisco–Oakland Bay Bridge, which had won federal financing. President Herbert Hoover named his former Stanford professor Charles Marx chair of the panel processing RFC applications. Drawing upon RFC funds, the federal government purchased a total of $71.4 million in two increments, allowing construction on the San Francisco–Oakland Bay Bridge to begin in May 1933.

Federal intervention of this level could not be repeated for a similar project on the same bay. The ferry companies unleashed a third wave of doubts, moreover—especially a renewed assault on the south pier site by geologist Robert Kinzie—that dimmed the confidence of RFC officials in the Golden Gate project. The Golden Gate Bridge and Highway District, meanwhile, was running out of operating funds, and there was little prospect of voters approving a third assessment, given the hesitancy of elected officials to go out on a limb, once again, for the Golden Gate Bridge project.

Enter Amadeo Peter Giannini, chairman and president of the Bank of America and the controlling presence on the Bankamerica syndicate that was considering the purchase of the $6 million in Golden Gate Bridge District bonds necessary to begin construction. At some point in time—most likely after the possibility of an RFC loan had collapsed—Joseph Strauss called on Giannini in Giannini's unpretentious office, open to an entire floor of other bankers and clerical staff at the Bank of America building at Powell and Market, which was Giannini's way of signaling to one and all his personal philosophy and practice of banking as a force for social development. Two visionaries were coming into each other's orbit, and the outcome of their conversation would be momentous.

Born in 1870 in San Jose, Giannini had learned the value of money, tragically, early in life. As a boy he had witnessed a farmhand shoot his father to death in a wage dispute over a matter of less than two dollars. Leaving school at fourteen, Giannini entered his stepfather's wholesale produce business and was by his thirties a wealthy man, on the lookout for further opportunities. Visiting Pasadena for a business conference, Giannini heard New Jersey governor Woodrow Wilson, the former president of Princeton turned Progressive reformer, criticize the exclusivity of American banking services, which Wilson described as a form of discrimination against the American consumer, who was also the American producer, hence the ultimate source of American wealth. Wilson's call for the extension of banking services to a wider clientele struck a chord in Giannini. In the course of his career as a wholesale buyer and seller of produce, Giannini had had ample opportunity to experience the vitality of family-owned and -operated

Bank of Italy (better known as Bank of America) founder Amadeo Peter Giannini saw in Strauss's Golden Gate Bridge a vehicle for the social and economic development of San Francisco and Northern California. Pictured here with granddaughters Anne (left) and Virginia (right) in a Moulin Studios portrait. *(Courtesy of the Bancroft Library, University of California, Berkeley)*

farms, together with the entrepreneurialism of small-scale produce jobbers. Joining the board of the Columbus Savings and Loan Society in San Francisco, Giannini entered the world of retail banking. He resigned in frustration, however, when his fellow board members rejected his pleas to lend money to working people and small businesses. In 1904 Giannini founded his own bank, the Bank of Italy, in the heavily Italian North Beach district of San Francisco.

It was the official beginning of a brilliant banking career that would see the Bank of Italy—the Bank of America after 1929—grow into a branch banking behemoth throughout California and, through the Transamerica Corporation, a force on the national scene. When earthquake and fire destroyed North Beach in April 1906, Giannini set up an outdoor office on a plank board supported by two barrels and made loans for the rebuilding of homes and businesses. Under his guidance, the Bank of America persuaded an entire generation of small depositors not to hoard savings in cash under a mattress but to deposit its hard-earned money with a local branch of the Bank of America. With the vast sums accumulated by the bank from depositors whom Giannini described as "the little guy," the Bank of America helped California accrue a local source of development capital that helped liberate California from its longtime status as an economic colony of eastern banks. A Progressive reformer throughout his life, Giannini believed that the deposits of working men and women and small business enterprises could create impressive pools of capital, and that this money, in turn, could be used for the social and economic development of California, which would, in turn, create more jobs, savings, and deposits. In this regard, the Bank of America helped finance the expansion of California agriculture and the rise of the motion picture industry, together with innumerable homes and smaller businesses.

When Joseph Strauss made his plea to the great banker—who would soon play a pivotal role in putting Franklin Delano Roosevelt into the White House—Giannini saw before him an entrepreneur, a visionary very much in his own mode. In the proposed Golden Gate Bridge, Giannini beheld a prophetic, if embattled, vehicle for the social and economic development of San Francisco and Northern California. Saying, "We'll take the bonds. We need the bridge," Giannini promised Strauss that Bank of America would purchase the first offering of bonds. When opponents of the Bridge project went to court to oppose the 5.25 percent rate of interest the Bank of America was requesting, Giannini agreed to accept a lower rate. As things turned out, the legal challenge to a higher rate failed, the 5.25 percent interest rate was reestablished, and the Bank of America financed the construction of the Golden Gate Bridge. How long would this bridge last, Giannini asked Strauss at the conclusion of their meeting? "Forever," Strauss replied.

-7-

DESIGN

Had Strauss's original design been built by 1927, as was first planned, it would have justified all charges by the Sierra Club and others that the Bridge would desecrate the site. "An upside-down rat trap" was one description offered by opponents. An undistinguished example of industrial design, Strauss's bridge would have scarred the majestic vista with a jumble of trussed steel towers and arrogant superstructures reaching out triangularly from their cantilevered base in support of an aesthetically overwhelmed suspension system. By late 1930 Strauss was displaying totally new designs for a pure suspension bridge, the longest on the planet, 4,200 feet from tower to tower:

a structure of grace and beauty, emanating an almost supernal amalgam of lightness and strength, its towers rising in Art Deco elegance against the California sky.

How did this happen? How was the upside-down rat trap, the steel cage, the clunky industrial hybrid, transformed into a work of engineering art? The answer—through the harmonized contributions of a team of noted engineering designers from across the nation and two architects—underscores Strauss's strengths and limitations. On the one hand, Strauss was able to lay aside his design when objections surfaced and recruit a top team of superior talents. On the other hand, as time would tell, Strauss would refuse to give credit where credit was due and would deliberately erase the contribution of the engineer critically responsible for the design of the suspension system.

As in the case of all public works, the design of the Golden Gate Bridge was driven by politics and cost. The incorporation of the Golden Gate Bridge and Highway District in December 1928 in no way assured Joseph Strauss that he would continue to lead the project. First of all, there was the dissatisfaction with his 1921 design. As early as May 1924, Los Angeles engineer Allan Rush, who had long been studying the challenge of bridging the Golden Gate, published an alternative solution: a suspension span anchored from two land-based concrete piers and towers on either side of the strait. Deficient in its navigational clearances, devoid of convincing engineering calculations in terms of its loads and stresses, Rush's futuristic design nevertheless trumped the Strauss proposal in the judgment of everyone who saw it and remained for the rest of the decade a dramatic warning that the Strauss design was woefully clumsy.

Then there was the matter of cost, which remained a point of contention throughout the 1920s as the Bridge project negotiated the political process. The original estimate of cost by Strauss and O'Shaughnessy was $17.25 million, later raised to $21 million. Opponents countered with estimates reaching as much as $100 million. Taking control of the Bridge District, president William Filmer, a San Francisco businessman with first-rate political connections, and newly appointed general manager Alan MacDonald, an equally well connected San Francisco contracting executive, faced two questions: How much would this bridge cost? And who should serve as chief engineer? Neither Filmer nor the other Bridge District directors, including San Francisco congressman Richard Welch, were in a mood to be manipulated by anyone, including Joseph Strauss. Over the course of the past decade, Strauss had revealed himself to many as not only a militant visionary but a difficult man as well, Napoleonic in ego, not a good listener or taker of direction from others. He was, moreover, Chicago based, not a local, given to intermittent absences on other business.

On the other hand, despite their reservations and their desire to nail down, once and for all, the cost of the project, the District board—comprised, as it was, of canny politicians—saw Strauss's value as an established spokesman, an avatar and publicist in whom the project had already invested costs of public relations capital and goodwill. City engineer Michael O'Shaughnessy, meanwhile, the original co-author of the Golden Gate Bridge proposal, was embroiled in controversy over cost overruns with the Hetch Hetchy project and had distanced himself from the Golden Gate Bridge scheme. At an earlier time in his career, O'Shaughnessy might have moved into the Bridge project as chief engineer, managing the talents of others, but given the cost overruns at Hetch Hetchy, he was fighting to save his reputation and career.

The strategy determined by the Bridge directors was straightforward: establish a board of engineering consultants—the finest in the nation—and have it report to the directors, thereby allowing the District to establish its own center of expertise and authority outside the jurisdiction of Strauss or anyone else who might be named chief engineer. Already, as early as 1922, bolstering the engineering capacity of his company (and, perhaps, at least tacitly acknowledging his own lack of expertise), Strauss had added to his Chicago staff as vice president for bridge design and construction Charles Alton Ellis, professor of structural and bridge engineering at the University of Illinois and, before that, an experienced design engineer in the private sector. Now, in the early weeks of organization of the Bridge District, Strauss, still in an acting capacity as chief engineer, got out ahead of the parade in the recruitment of national talent and began the process of making contacts on behalf of the board. However risky, Strauss's strategy worked, and by late 1929 Strauss was ensconced on the fourth floor of the Russ Building in the downtown, confirmed as chief engineer and listing on his stationery a panel of engineering consultants that included the best talent in the nation.

First of all, listed as designing engineer, was Ellis, fifty-three, a Maine-born Yankee, modest and unassuming in manner, passionately devoted to ancient history and classical Greek literature, which he read in the original. Ellis's key gift as a bridge designer and civil engineer was his fluency, genius even, in the mathematical analysis of structural challenges: his expertise, for example, in analyzing the stresses on subway tubes under the Hudson River on behalf of the American Bridge Company, which he joined in 1902. Leaving American Bridge in 1908, Ellis joined the faculty of the University of Michigan, followed by a two-year stint as designing engineer for the Dominion Bridge Company, followed in turn, in 1916, by promotion to professor of structural and bridge engineering at the University of Illinois. Ellis, in short, showed that mixture of active and academic involvement characteristic of engineering and architecture in the early years of the twentieth century. Despite his mathematical and mechanical expertise and his authorship of the standard textbook on framed structures, Ellis resisted a full-time academic career. In 1921 he left the University of Illinois to join the Strauss Engineering Corporation of Chicago.

The three consulting engineers on the Golden Gate Bridge and Highway District panel included the leading theoretician of suspension bridge design in the nation, fifty-seven-year-old Leon Moisseiff. Born in Riga, Latvia, and educated there at the Baltic Polytechnic Institute, Moisseiff immigrated with his family to the United States at nineteen and took his degree in civil engineering from Columbia in 1895. By 1929, when he joined the Golden Gate Bridge project, Moisseiff, an independent consultant—residually European in manner, throughout life wearing the imperial mustache and goatee of the fin de siècle—had earned a reputation as a bridge designer (the Manhattan Bridge [1909] over the East River, the Benjamin Franklin Bridge [1926] across the Delaware) and the leading theoretician of a new kind of suspension bridge, employing slender steel towers in place of bulky stone and concrete, designs based on fresh calculations by Moisseiff regarding wind shear and load stresses in a more flexible steel system. Already, as in the

Before the Bridge: A glimpse of the ocean beyond the mouth of the Golden Gate. *The Golden Gate, Looking West*, lithography by L. Prang & Co., ca. 1873, from a painting by John Ross Key. COURTESY OF THE BANCROFT LIBRARY, UNIVERSITY OF CALIFORNIA, BERKELEY.

Another nineteenth-century image of the Golden Gate, this one from the west, depicting Fort Point on the near shore and the Marin Headlands in the distance. Illustration by Danish artist Peter Petersen Toft.

COURTESY OF THE BANCROFT LIBRARY, UNIVERSITY OF CALIFORNIA, BERKELEY.

Ray Strong's famous painting of the Bridge captured a very early stage
construction from the San Francisco side of the span. His bright colors and liv
lines capture something of the Golden Gate's dynamism, even with the Brid
scarcely begun. STRONG, *GOLDEN GATE BRIDGE*, 1934. OIL ON CANVAS. SMITHSONIAN AMERICAN /
MUSEUM, WASHINGTON, D.C./ART RESOURCE, NY.

tailed view of the cable saddle atop the south tower of the Bridge.

A 1948 American Airlines poster by Edward McKnight Kauffer gives the Bridge a minimalist treatment, but indicates how quickly it became a national symbol the Bay Area. © K.J. HISTORICAL/CORBIS.

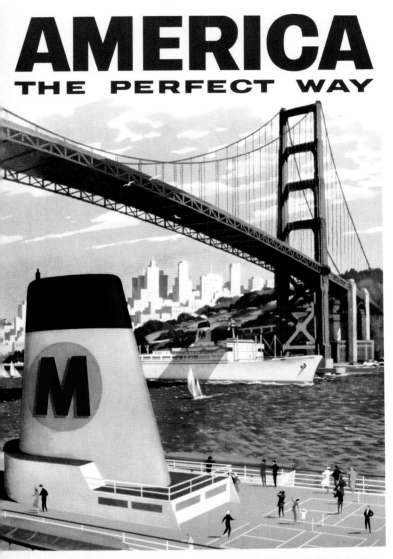

AMERICA
THE PERFECT WAY

ᔆᔆMARIPOSA · ᔆᔆMONTEREY
Matson Lines

nother advertising poster captures the radiant International Orange of
ᴴe Bridge. *America the Perfect Way*, Matson Lines poster, ca. 1952.

In this view from inside Fort Point, the steel tracery of the Bridge seems to vau into space above the massive arches of the fort. COURTESY OF THE LIBRARY OF CONGRE HISTORIC AMERICAN BUILDINGS SURVEY COLLECTION.

affic on the Bridge at dawn. As of 2009, more than 1.8 billion vehicles have ssed the Bridge. COURTESY OF THE LIBRARY OF CONGRESS HISTORIC AMERICAN ENGINEERING CORD COLLECTION.

This aerial view from the south tower emphasizes its sinuous curves.

case of Ellis, Strauss had called upon Moisseiff's expertise in 1925 to confirm an estimated budget of $21 million for the Golden Gate Bridge proposal.

Moisseiff was the leading theoretician on the panel; Ellis, the leading mathematician. The third member, Othmar Hermann Ammann, fifty, designer of the George Washington Bridge (1931) then under construction across the Hudson, was equally legendary. Born in Switzerland in 1879 and educated at the Zurich Polytechnikum under the renowned Swiss engineer Wilhelm Ritter, Ammann immigrated to New York in 1904 and in that city, with its large German-speaking immigrant population, earned over the years an international reputation. Coming first to public notice as the author of the report on the failure of the Quebec Bridge in 1907, Ammann joined the staff of the respected bridge designer Gustav Lindenthal and was in 1925 appointed bridge engineer to the Port Authority of New York and New Jersey. As designer and supervising engineer, Ammann would bring the George Washington Bridge to completion six months ahead of schedule and under budget. Across his long career, working for the Port Authority or the Triborough Bridge and Tunnel Authority headed by Robert Moses, Ammann would design six major New York City bridges. Ammann's Verrazano-Narrows Bridge (1964) would ultimately surpass the Golden Gate Bridge by sixty feet as the longest single-span suspension bridge on the planet.

The fourth member of the Golden Gate Bridge and Highway District panel, Charles Derleth Jr., fifty-five, was the best-known engineer in the San Francisco Bay Area, involved directly or as a consultant with the construction of many of the major dams, highways, tunnels, and bridges in the Bay Area in the first three decades of the twentieth century, most recently the Carquinez Strait Highway Bridge (1920), for which he served as chief engineer. New York born, a graduate of City College and Columbia, where he took his civil engineering degree in 1896 and taught until 1901, Derleth pursued a hybrid career of academic and active consultant, based out of the University of California at Berkeley, where he had served as professor and dean of the College of Engineering since 1907. A well-known clubman and member of the San Francisco establishment, Derleth was associated with such projects as the Panama-Pacific International Exposition, the San Francisco Civic Center and Auditorium (which he also designed), and Grace Cathedral atop Nob Hill, together with the engineering design and construction of such signature Cal Berkeley buildings as California, Wheeler, Le Conte, and Gilman halls, the Doe Library, and the landmark campanile. A close friend of Robert Sproul, president of the university, Derleth served as chief spokesperson for Sproul's and the UC community's enthusiastic support for the Golden Gate Bridge. As soon as the Bridge and Highway

District was formed, Derleth made inquiries to general manager Alan MacDonald regarding his own candidacy as chief engineer (Leon Moisseiff was also being mentioned) but, outmaneuvered by Strauss, accepted membership on the panel of engineers instead, confident in his ability to exercise influence as engineer of choice for the local establishment.

Another UC Berkeley professor crucial to Strauss's team was the respected geologist Andrew Lawson. Sixty-eight at the time, Lawson—born in Scotland, raised in Canada, holding a PhD from Johns Hopkins, on the Berkeley faculty since 1890 after a stint with the Geological Survey of Canada—had made his reputation as the first geologist to map the entire length of the San Andreas Fault. As the author of the official report (1908) on the San Francisco earthquake of April 1906, commonly known as the Lawson Report, he had achieved even further fame. At the time of his recruitment by Strauss, Lawson had recently retired as professor of mineralogy and geology at Berkeley but remained active as a consultant into his eighties. He was an Edwardian gentleman with a walrus mustache, given to tweedy Norfolk jackets, living in a Craftsman home in the Berkeley hills designed for him by his friend the noted Bay Area architect Bernard Maybeck.

Two architects, John Eberson, fifty-four, and Irving Morrow, forty-five, played crucial roles as part of the design team; indeed, without them, the Bridge would not have reached the levels it did as a work of art. Neither man had any record in bridge design. Selected initially by Strauss, John Eberson of Chicago was the leading architect of motion picture theaters in the golden age of movie palaces. Eberson was, in fact, as Ruritarian and outré as any of the theaters he designed. Born in 1875 in Romania and educated in Dresden and at the University of Vienna, Eberson fled to the United States in the late 1890s, having escaped from a military prison, where he was serving time for disrespect to a senior officer. Settling in St. Louis—like New York, a decidedly German-speaking city—Eberson entered architecture as stage designer and illustrator of real estate posters and sales brochures. By the time he moved to Chicago in 1910, he had developed an impressive practice as a stage and theater designer. Over the next two decades, in a series of major commissions for the Loew's and Orpheum theater chains and freestanding clients, Eberson perfected what he described as "the Atmospheric Theater." By this he meant movie palaces in which the screen seemed to float in its own space, the pit orchestra rose from and descended to some mysterious region, and muraled walls glowed in opalescent color from indirect lighting, while carved ceilings and strategically placed vases and statuary suggested a Ruritanian environment suitable to an operetta by Emmerich Kálmán or Franz Lehár.

The very fact that Strauss initially chose Eberson to stylize the towers and other aspects of the structure underscores Strauss's sense of the Golden Gate Bridge as, in part, a theatrical production orchestrating site, structure, and atmospherics into a unified aesthetic statement. When Eberson, having completed preliminary renderings, asked for more money to finish the project, Strauss—partly upon the recommendation of San Francisco artist Maynard Dixon, who would himself play an indirect but relevant role in the stylization of the Bridge—turned to local architect Irving Morrow. Born in Oakland in 1884, Morrow graduated from Berkeley and in a rite of passage common to Bay Area architects at the time attended the École des Beaux-Arts in Paris and, in a further rite of passage, had worked on the Panama-Pacific International Exposition of 1915. A protégé of John Galen Howard, architect of the Berkeley campus and the planned development of St. Francis Wood in San Francisco, Morrow spent the years between 1915 and 1930 building a solid reputation, in partnership after 1925 with his wife Gertrude Comfort Morrow, the supervising architect of St. Francis Wood. Morrow worked as a general designer of homes, schools, hotels, theaters, and commercial buildings, a landscape architect, and an editor and writer for *Pacific Coast Architecture*, *Architectural Record*, and other periodicals, and his architectural tastes, informed by personal scholarship, evolved with the times, moving from Beaux-Arts to Mediterranean Revival to, at the time Strauss retained him in 1930, Art Deco.

Meeting at the Alta Mira Hotel in Sausalito in late August 1929 for the first time as a group, the engineering board commenced the awesome task of designing the longest suspension bridge ever to be attempted to that time. Like the Bridge it created, the design team for the Golden Gate Bridge—by its diversity of Jewish and Christian origins (Latvia, Romania, Switzerland, the United States), the great universities and polytechnics it represented (Vienna, Zurich, the École des Beaux-Arts, Columbia, Johns Hopkins, Illinois, Berkeley), the places of business and residences of its principals (New York, Chicago, the San Francisco Bay Area), and the national reach of what had already been accomplished—signaled, if only accidentally, an inclusive range of backgrounds expressive of the forces of immigration, population, and professional practice being funneled into the creation of the nation itself in the first three decades of the twentieth century.

Strauss began the design process by asking Professor Lawson of Berkeley to resolve once and for all the persistently troublesome issue of the geological suitability of the site. Strauss treated the testing by land- or barge-based diamond drills under Lawson's supervision of the geology of the anchorage and pier sites, especially the contested site of the southern pier, as a soft opening for the entire construction process. There were speeches from a platform filled with notables, a band played, and a local radio station provided live coverage. Fortunately, the drilling had positive results, although Lawson required some coaching from Derleth to express his findings as strongly as possible, without academic qualification. Derleth himself, a designer of bridges and dams, would in time direct his expertise to the massive concrete and steel anchorages and piers upon which the Bridge rested. Ammann, meanwhile, the most experienced bridge designer and builder of them all, played a continuing role in consulting on the assembling of the various components of the bridge—anchorages, piers, towers, supporting cables, suspension cables dropping to the roadbed, entrance and exit ways in San Francisco and Marin—into functional unity. Each of these components was discernible in terms of its individual engineering and its interaction with the rest as a whole. Towers rose from piers. Cables arched across towers toward anchorages. The roadbed hung suspended from support lines. But the designers of the Golden Gate Bridge were facing a more difficult problem. Could such a bridge—light, graceful, soaring across its space in a gentle arc—be engineered in the first place?

Enter Leon Moisseiff and Charles Alton Ellis. The defining feature of the Golden Gate Bridge, now that Strauss's hybrid solution had been abandoned, would be its suspension system. As evident in the George Washington Bridge now under construction, the theory and design of suspension systems—thanks in sufficient measure to three members of the Golden Gate Bridge board, Moisseiff, Ammann, and Ellis—was in a state of rapid development. Spanning 3,500 feet from two 604-foot towers at shoreline, the George Washington Bridge would by its completion be the longest suspension bridge on the planet. Moisseiff had worked as theoretician and consulting designer for the George Washington Bridge, as well as, before that, for the Benjamin Franklin Bridge (1926), originally called the Philadelphia–Camden Bridge across the Delaware River, the second-longest suspension bridge in the world as of 1929. Both Moisseiff and Ellis, however, knew that the Golden Gate presented a greater challenge. Across the strait, from tower to tower, they were facing a greater distance, 4,200 feet in all. The tidal action of the strait, moreover, far exceeded that of the Hudson or the Delaware. It was, in point of fact, at 2.3 million cubic feet per second at high tide, one of the most powerful tidal movements on earth. As far as weather was concerned, a prevailing wind blew in a westerly direction, down through the strait as through a wind tunnel. At gale force, these winds could reach up to seventy miles per hour. Persistent fog banks would not only corrode the steel structure over time, they would also—given the intermittent sunshine—subject the steel of the structure to expansion and contraction on a regular basis. Then there was the danger, the inevitability even, of earthquakes. Centered on the San Andreas Fault, the earthquake of April 1906 had been 8.3 on the Richter scale. How much of an earthquake the prospective bridge could be engineered to withstand remained a troubling question. The Golden Gate Bridge, in short, would be required not only to be the longest suspension bridge in the world, it would also be required to possess the strength and flexibility of a great ship at sea, enduring gale force winds, as well as being a land-based structure capable of withstanding recurrent tremors in the earth, eventually even that great earthquake that all Bay Area residents, however subconsciously, realized would one day again strike their region. And finally, the Bridge would have to be beautiful, very beautiful, to be worthy of the beauty of the Marin Headlands, the Pacific, and the pastel Atlantis rising on the shore of the Bay.

All this would require state-of-the-art theories and designs of engineering and, when it came to the towers, architecture well beyond the abilities of Joseph Strauss, the chief engineer. With some rapidity Strauss turned the design of the suspension system, which is to say, the very essence of the Bridge, over to his vice president for bridge design at Strauss Engineering. "I can have Professor Ellis adjust matters" was the way that Strauss characterized the assignment. "Mr. Strauss gave me some pencils" was the way that Ellis would later describe his commission. Two days after the Sausalito meeting, Strauss headed east for a two-month absence on other business, leaving Ellis behind in San Francisco to manage the project.

By March 1930 the engineering board had decided upon its design program: an all-suspension bridge, its steel towers rising from two piers, one 1,100 feet off the San Francisco shore, the other on the Marin shoreline. By locating the south, or San Francisco, pier offshore, the length of the necessary suspension system, as great as it was, would be kept to a minimum; and there would be no need to tear down the historic Fort Point (1857), which Strauss especially wanted to preserve. Instead, a great steel arch, a bridge within the bridge, would soar over Fort Point out to the south tower. Unlike the San Francisco–Oakland Bay Bridge, the Golden Gate Bridge would not accommodate interurban electrics, which in any event were not operating in the sparsely settled North Bay.

Returning to Chicago and New York from the March 1930 San Francisco meeting, Ellis and Moisseiff got to work on the suspension system. Challenged by Moisseiff's notion that suspension bridges could be made lighter and more slender and still bear the same loads as heavier structures, Ellis spent the next twenty months—communicating with Moisseiff by telegram—evolving, designing, and mathematically testing a suspension system, light and aerodynamic in comparison to previous suspension bridges yet possessed of superior load capacity. For Ellis to achieve such an advancement in the art of bridge design required a harmonization of theory and practice. The theory came from Moisseiff, Ellis, and others on the engineering board. The practice was, first of all, in the design of the suspension system itself, with Ellis doing the heavy lifting in consultation with Moisseiff. But the design process by definition demanded testing. Prototypes and engineering theory could point the way, but as a design challenge and concept the Golden Gate Bridge was operating out ahead of theory and prototype. There was only one way for Ellis to test his conclusions—through mathematics. A bridge could not be built to see if it worked. It would have to be tested through mathematics before it was built. This is exactly what Ellis did in those twenty months: fuse into one design solution, mathematically calculated, the capacities of a man-made structure subjected to complex forces of natural action and material substance.

First of all, there was the basic question of load. How much load could the Bridge be designed for, and how could this load be distributed throughout the entire system? Then there was the question of the parts of the Bridge relating to the function of the whole. Acting as a unified system, like the parts of a ship at sea, the Bridge was a system in motion under changing pressures greater than the sum of its parts.

The slenderized towers, for example, would sway in four directions because of wind or variations in load, and this in turn would require, at any given moment, ongoing adjustments throughout the entire system. Heat or cold could expand or contract steel. Thus changes in weather would demand comparable adjustments. For all its apparent solidity, the Bridge was a system in motion. Articulated through mathematical calculation, design had simultaneously to deal with permanence and flux, and Ellis faced this paradox as he performed his heroic calculations on blank paper in that pre-computer age in his Chicago office, in the study of his home in Evanston, or on trains to and from San Francisco.

In *The Golden Gate Bridge* (1937), the final report on the Bridge and its construction to the directors of the Bridge and Highway District, Strauss presented a section dealing with the mathematics behind the preliminary design. By this, Strauss meant Ellis's mathematics, although Ellis was not mentioned by name. To the layman, examining these pages today, these simultaneous equations, parading across the page in Arabic numerals, Greek and Latin letters, lines, brackets, parentheses, and computational signs, constitute hieroglyphics possessed of a near-mystical power, unlocking the realities of nature itself. Ellis was a classicist by avocation, a student of ancient Greek; and there was something Pythagorean and Platonic in what he was attempting through Number, the deciphering of nature's secrets.

Born on the island of Samos some 580 years prior to the Common Era, Pythagoras was himself a mystic, a philosopher, and a mathematician whose theorem that the square on the hypotenuse of a right-angle triangle is equal to the sum of the squares of the two other sides would continue to challenge and torment high school students for the two and a half millennia to come. On a more mystical level, Pythagoras—who might have been influenced by Indian philosophy in this regard—rejected the notion that mathematics constituted merely a man-made tool for analysis. Number, rather, was a direct revelation of the structure of creation itself. Knowing Number, the mind knew Nature; and knowing Nature—knowing Nature completely, that is—the mind knew Number, for it was Number that kept Nature in existence. The mathematics of music, Pythagoras believed, came closest to revealing this reality, for the universe itself, in the movement of its stars and planets, yielded cosmic harmony and song.

Influenced by Pythagoras, Plato would develop Number into Idea, possessed of the same prior ontology; and Pythagoras's notion that the spheres made music as they moved through the heavens remained, along with Platonism, a staple of Western thought down through the Renaissance. As Galileo, the Cambridge Platonists, Sir Isaac Newton, and so many other scientists of the Renaissance and Enlightenment asserted, empirical science, based in observation and Number, could not completely account for the mystery of things, which classical Greek philosophy had never forgot. The Seven Wonders of the Ancient World emanated such great power not only because they fulfilled practical needs or expressed grand social and cultural ambitions but because as well they suggested, through design, through engineering, through beauty, a sense of something more, edging into the realms of religion, philosophy, and art.

To suggest that all this was on Charles Alton Ellis's mind as he performed his calculations would be presumptuous. Ellis was a professional engineer, doing a professional engineer's work, designing a bridge. But we do know of Ellis's love of Greek civilization, and we do know of his engineering and mathematical expertise, and we do have the continuing presence of the Bridge he envisioned and helped bring into being, a masterpiece of engineering and art made possible through Number, just as Pythagoras or Plato would have understood it.

Joseph Strauss, however, was not impressed. Ellis, Strauss believed, was taking too long to perform the calculations, and so in November 1931 Strauss wrote a letter removing Ellis from the project. The following month, again by letter, Strauss fired Ellis from the company. He had been exaggerating the time and expense of computing the suspension system, Strauss wrote Ellis. He should turn over his papers and calculations to the office, where a subordinate would finish them with dispatch. The man most responsible for the engineering design of the Golden Gate Bridge had just been fired.

Fortunately, Strauss proved less threatened, hence more patient, when it came to highlighting and heightening the art of the Bridge, including the selection of its color. The art, of course, was inseparable from the engineering, and so Ellis, Moisseiff, Ammann, Derleth, and all the other engineers attached to the project must be allowed to share credit for the art of the Golden Gate Bridge: Moisseiff especially, who preached lightness, and Ellis, who made such lightness possible. But so much of the artfulness of the Golden Gate Bridge comes from its towers, and here Joseph Strauss, once again, inserted himself into the process when he contacted John Eberson to make the towers, through architectural design, a key component of the Bridge's artistic success. With the fervor of a convert, Strauss was now looking for something more than unadorned industrialism in his two 746-foot towers. He wanted theater, drama, grandeur, even the mysterious, and so he turned to Eberson, just as the engineers of the Boulder-Hoover Dam were turning to architect Gordon Kaufmann to stylize the hydroelectric intake towers, and the California Toll Bridge Authority would soon be turning to San Francisco architect Timothy

Pflueger for remedial stylization of the four towers of the San Francisco—Oakland Bay Bridge.

Eberson set the tone and established the preliminary designs. The Golden Gate Bridge would have to it an element of theater. Building on Eberson's suggestions, Irving Morrow finished the task. Interestingly enough, it was an artist, Maynard Dixon, and not an engineer or an architect who recommended Morrow to Strauss and the District. At the time, Dixon was doing an oil portrait of the Bridge, not yet built, from imagination and from the unusual perspective of looking down at the roadbed from the tower, with the cables and suspension system dominating the view. While developing his talents as an artist, Dixon had served a crucial stint as an illustrator in Los Angeles for Foster & Kleiser, then in the process of developing the billboard as an advertising medium. A billboard, like a bridge, must be experienced from a moving automobile as well as from a stabilized distance; hence it must make its statement as vividly and directly as possible. Again like a bridge, a billboard is seen against the sky; hence its delineations and colors must be bold and assertive, with background kept to a minimum. Turning to murals in the 1920s, Dixon would make these Foster & Kleiser precepts of immediacy, clear design, and color the fundamental foundations and premises of his success. For the time being, he was also thinking about them in conjunction with the Golden Gate Bridge.

So too did Dixon's good friend Irving Morrow appreciate the scenic. Morrow was himself, in fact, a skilled illustrator, as his preliminary charcoal drawings of a not-yet-built Golden Gate Bridge suggested. Eberson established an Art Deco design vocabulary for the towers. Like the great Art Deco skyscrapers of the era, the towers would be stepped back in volume and silhouette. By stepping the towers back as they ascended, Eberson was not only responding to Moisseiff's notion that suspension bridge towers could be slenderized, he was also responding to a fundamental characteristic of the Chrysler Building in New York, among other examples, or the entrances and porte cocheres of the Art Deco theaters, hotels, and medical and business buildings of the period.

In improving upon Eberson's suggestions, Morrow intensified Eberson's Art Deco styling of the towers by further accentuating the stepped-back segments rising vertically on all sides. Morrow also squared off the fourth and final top opening in each tower, which Eberson had kept rounded to resemble a proscenium arch. Morrow also covered all four cross-bracings above the Bridge deck with chevron-shaped plates of vertical fluting, and placed decorative non-structural steel brackets in fourteen corners. Cast as stepped-backed layered geometric shapes, these decorative brackets reinforced the Art Deco effect of the tower. Thanks to their height and their Art Deco styling, then, each tower communicated a sense of geometric rhythms, repetitions, and tensions harmonized into dynamic repose. The cable suspension of the roadbed at the one-third point of each tower, finally, 220 feet above the water, allowed the towers to soar unimpeded for the remaining two thirds of their 746-foot height against the skyline.

Suspended from each tower were the reversed vertical arches of the two great support cables, the largest ever spun, from which hung 250 pairs of steel suspender ropes spaced fifty feet apart. Seen from a distance, the tower cables, suspender ropes, and roadbed, which rose in its center in a gentle curve, defined the overall structure of the Bridge. Seen from an automobile, the towers rose from the roadbed as predominant structures, experienced separately as sculptured monuments heroic in scale, sometimes clearly seen against the sky, or their heights, even their midsections, absorbed into a bank of fog. Perceived from an even farther distance—offshore, for example, or from the Berkeley hills—the Bridge boldly integrated city, sea, sky, and headlands into a total composition.

It was able to do this, finally—reinforce its unity as an engineered and sculptured structure harmonizing bridge, site, and atmospherics—because of a crucial design decision that came only later during the construction process. Color.

O. H. Ammann favored gray, as used for the George Washington Bridge. Some wanted black. The Navy preferred a yellow and black striping to facilitate visibility for ships entering or leaving the Gate through low-lying fog. The Army Air Corps liked the stripes idea but preferred a red and white color scheme more visible from the air. While the Bridge was under construction, however, a reddish lead-based primer—sometimes known as International Orange—was used to protect the rising structure against the elements. Lo and behold, the more the debate raged as to what colors to use to paint the Bridge, the more competitive became its temporary primer. No one intended this at the time, but this color, International Orange, had strong linkages to one of the staple colors in the color scheme employed by scenic colorist Jules Guerin for the Panama-Pacific International Exhibition of 1915 as being, in Guerin's opinion, most suitable to the topography, vegetation, and atmospherics of the bayside Harbor View site. Black would have fought site and vista to a deadly standstill. Gray would have yielded to the fog without a contest. A striped solution, whether yellow or red, would have fragmented the total unity of bridge design. International Orange, by contrast, had already suggested its compatibility as far as site and atmospherics were concerned. It also further unified the Bridge into one compelling statement. And more, in the depth psychology of color itself, International Orange bespoke the gold of the Golden Gate, the gold of the Gold Rush that had created the Bay Area, and the gold of the Golden Horn of the Bosporus first suggested by John Charles Frémont when he named the site in 1846 and by metaphor evoked a color-drenched city of towers, domes, and stepped-back structures rising like Constantinople from blue waters along green hillsides, their red-tiled roofs touching a sun-flooded azure sky.

-8-

CONSTRUCTION

Such a construction project, on such a monumental scale, involving such an intricate interplay of construction technology and human skill, required an equally intricate interplay of labor and management at all levels of supervision and work. Just as the design of the Bridge had been a team effort, so too was the management of the construction enterprise. As usual, Joseph Strauss played impresario and chief spokesman. Wearing a slouch hat, his double-breasted overcoat draped poetically over his shoulders, Strauss made grand entrances to and exits from the construction site, Sol Hurok on a Hollywood set, Frank Lloyd Wright conferring with clients. But Strauss had never supervised the construction of a suspension bridge, even a small one, and he needed an on-site supervising engineer, a construction boss, with experience, and so with typical chutzpah Strauss turned to a student of the very man he had recently fired, Charles Alton Ellis, whose contribution to the Bridge Strauss would do his best to erase from memory.

In his mid-thirties when first contacted by Strauss in 1932, Russell Cone epitomized the accomplishment and panache of the World War I generation, now in the full tide of its influence and achievement. Iowa born, Cone had served with the famed Rainbow Division during the war. Following his release from the service, he took a civil engineering degree in bridge design at the University of Illinois, studying with Ellis, whom he admired enormously. The two became colleagues and friends as Cone rose rapidly in the world of suspension bridge construction, serving as resident engineer on, among other projects, the Ambassador and Benjamin Franklin bridges. In the movie that might have been made, Cone would be best played by Spencer Tracy: bluff, direct, physically courageous, never asking his men to work anywhere that he himself would not go, a drinking buddy of Chicago newsman Charles MacArthur of *The Front Page* fame: a character out of *The Front Page*, in fact, in his midwestern unpretentiousness and breezy optimism.

No wonder Strauss wanted Cone as supervising engineer, offering to double his salary to $10,000 a year. Cone was everything Strauss was not: credentialed yet hands-on, a man's man, capable of gaining the respect of ironworkers and other construction types. Still, Strauss had a well-earned reputation for being difficult, and for a while Cone resisted. Here was the man, after all, who had fired his favorite professor. Yet the prospect of supervising the construction of the greatest suspension bridge in human history proved impossible to resist, and by February 1933 Cone and his family were heading west to San Francisco.

Once again, there Cone would encounter a new player on the management scene, James Reed, a retired Navy commander, recently general manager of Schlage Lock, who had replaced Alan MacDonald as general manager of the Bridge and Highway District. Solidly backed by the San Francisco business establishment, Reed was tough-minded, alert to managerial politics, exacting in the manner of a commanding officer at sea. Tightening District control, Reed personally reviewed and approved all contracts and reports and reinforced the role of Berkeley professor Charles Derleth as the District's man on the board of engineers. Strauss, in turn, faced with such formidable players at District headquarters and on-site, strengthened the role of his executive vice president and aide-de-camp, Clifford Paine. Born in 1887 and raised in rural Michigan, Paine took his engineering degree from the University of

Michigan and went to work for the American Bridge Company. His odd-couple relationship to Strauss began when Strauss demanded that Paine be fired from American Bridge as a result of a bidding dispute, one of Strauss's many quarrels with clients and competitors. Five months later, American Bridge rehired Paine, and once again Paine came to Strauss's attention, this time when Paine discovered a major miscalculation in the course of reviewing plans from the Strauss Company for the Black Rock Channel Bridge in Buffalo. Saved by Paine from an embarrassing, possibly disastrous error, Strauss reversed course and this time hired Paine for his own company. Not for long, however. Discovering that Paine had patented a new kind of vertical-lift bridge employing synchronized motors, Strauss asked Paine, his employee, for the rights to use the design. Fearing that Strauss would hijack his patent, Paine refused and was once again fired. Following service as a first lieutenant in the Corps of Engineers in World War I, Paine distinguished himself as a designer of vertical-lift and railroad bridges. In 1921 Strauss rehired Paine as his chief designing engineer.

One need not be Sigmund Freud to see in the Strauss-Paine relationship deep currents of mutual need. Once again, Strauss was appropriating the talents of a better-trained engineer. Emotional, egomaniacal, by turns quarrelsome and cunning, Strauss was a master politician. On the other hand, Paine was the perfect second in command. Reserved, modest, a Michigan farm boy in the great world, Paine loathed the politics of engineering projects. Psychologically, as his own complexities became more debilitating, Strauss grew to depend more and more upon Paine as his alter ego, the quiet and steady presence he could never be.

When Strauss fired Ellis, he put Paine in charge of finishing Ellis's report, despite the fact that Paine was only peripherally familiar with suspension engineering. As construction of the Golden Gate Bridge proceeded, Strauss—suffering from yet another bout of withdrawal from the scene that had characterized his career—was, when in San Francisco, spending more and more time in his Nob Hill apartment, observing the spinning of cables through a telescope in a manner eerily similar to how John Roebling, debilitated by caisson disease (the bends), observed the final phases of the construction of the Brooklyn Bridge via telescope from his apartment, in the same room in which Hart Crane lived when observing the Brooklyn Bridge and writing his great poem in the mid- to late 1920s.

Yet if Strauss was, on occasion, unexplainably absent, Clifford Paine was ceaselessly and tirelessly present on the construction site. While Strauss, ensconced in his Nob Hill apartment, was seen primarily at Bridge District meetings, and then only as a near-silent, enigmatic presence, Clifford Paine was everywhere, climbing ladders and catwalks, inspecting every aspect of the job, improving the designs for the suspender ropes, dealing with the paint issue, writing the necessary reports. In October 1935, in yet one more breakdown of communication, Paine threatened to resign. Strauss made Paine his equal partner and renamed the firm Strauss & Paine, Incorporated.

Construction on the Golden Gate Bridge began on January 5, 1933. Three years and five months later, on May 27, 1937, the newly completed Bridge was ceremonially opened to pedestrian traffic. During these forty-one months, an epic of construction was played out. Like all epics, the construction of the Golden Gate Bridge constituted an heroic narrative of historical and personal event. Like all epics as well, building the Bridge, spanning the Gate, was possessed of multiple meanings. It was, simultaneously, a marvel of engineering construction, a testimony to the private sector on a local and national basis, a model of public sector sponsorship, a healing therapy in the midst of economic depression, and a testimony to the skills, resilience, inventiveness, and courage of the American worker.

Prior to construction, the Golden Gate Bridge had been envisioned, politically energized, legislatively empowered, organized as a district, geologically verified, engineered, and designed. Now ensued the ten phases of the construction process: the definition of tasks, the awarding of contracts, the laying down of foundations, the erection of towers, the spinning and installation of cables, the suspension of the roadway structure, the paving of the road-bed, the installation of lighting and other electrical systems, the clearing and paving of access roadways and tunnels in San Francisco and Marin, the design and construction of a toll plaza. Each phase presented distinctive challenges to the public and private sectors, supervising engineers, and the workers making it all happen. Taken in its totality—perceived, that is, as an integrated process—the construction of the Golden Gate Bridge constituted in one dimension of its multiple meanings a milestone of American achievement at a time when such an acting out of American expertise and resilience was sorely necessary. Until the very end of the process, it looked as if it would be an epic unmarred by tragedy. But there is no such thing as an epic innocent of tragedy and loss, and the Golden Gate Bridge would prove no exception.

Who were the companies awarded the contract, hence challenged to create this unprecedented feat of engineering? Adding their corporate identities to the multiple meanings of the Bridge, they were at once local, national, and, in the case of one company, profoundly historic. Given the pervasiveness of the Depression, it is not surprising that Bay Area–based companies claimed an edge when it came to the bidding process. The project, after all, was a local project, under the supervision of a localized Bridge and Highway District, set in motion by local taxes, and financed by a syndicate headed up by the San Francisco–based Bank of America. The awarding of each contract showed local versus national tensions. When the bidding wars were over, West Coast companies were awarded approximately $7.5 million of the $24 million in construction contracts. Barrett & Hilp won the contract for the cable anchorages and piers for the approach spans. The Pacific Bridge Company would build the strait-based San Francisco pier and fender and the land-based pier in Marin. J. H. Pomeroy & Company and the Raymond Concrete Pile Company would have responsibility for the approach spans on either shore. Eaton & Smith would build the Presidio-side approach roads. (The Marin approach roads and tunnel were separately financed and supervised by the state Division of Highways.) The Alta Electric & Mechanical Company would be responsible for electric construction and installation. These were local companies with solid reputations, coming in lowest in the bidding process.

The $10.7 million contract for seventy-five thousand tons of fabricated steel, however, and the $5.9 million contract for cables, suspenders, and suspension accessories proved more controversial. As might be expected, the San Francisco Labor Council and other Bay Area interests wanted as much of the steel contract as possible. The problem was the West Coast had no heavy steel fabricating plant (and would not until Henry J. Kaiser created one in Southern California in 1942). The giant in the field was the fabricated steel construction division of Bethlehem Steel, based in Pennsylvania. Within the last decade, Bethlehem Steel had built twelve important American bridges, including four state-of-the-art suspension structures: the Ambassador (1929) in Detroit, the Mount Hope (1929) linking Portsmouth and Bristol, Rhode Island, the Anthony Wayne (1931) in Toledo, and the George Washington (1931) in New York. Recognizing this, local interests angled for as much of the steel business as possible—approximately five hundred tons of handrails and portal bracings—to be fabricated in the one small mill Bethlehem maintained in South San Francisco and for the steel fabricated in Bethlehem, Pennsylvania, and Sparrows Point, Maryland, shipped from the East via the Panama Canal, to be stored and further prepared for use, as far as possible, in local warehouses.

The spinning of cables and the installation of the suspension system, however, involved a more complicated process. The first low bidder for the contract was the American Cable Company of Monessen, Pennsylvania, but only on the condition that the Reconstruction Finance Corporation finance the project. When that effort failed, the District called for new bids in the fall of 1932, and among the lowest bidders were the E. H. Edwards Company of San Francisco, the diversely based Columbia Steel Company, and the John A. Roebling's Sons Company of New York. As a local enterprise, the E. H. Edwards Company had its backers but failed to convince the District that it had the capacity for such an ambitious program. Columbia Steel maintained a plant in Pittsburg on the Carquinez Strait and had strong local support, including the San Francisco Chamber of Commerce, but was underbid—by a mere $31,000—by the Roebling Company, which as part of its bid package promised to construct a plant in the Bay Area and to spend half of its money locally. The selection of Roebling not only gave the contract to the lowest bidder, it brought to the construction of the cables and suspension system the company that had built the Brooklyn Bridge more than a half century earlier.

Located on solid rock, the anchorages for the Bridge cables, north and south, presented a straightforward construction challenge: Clear the site down to bedrock and level it out. Drive down a steel foundation. Build a steel plate and wooden mold and construct within it a network of reinforcing steel bars. Anchor sixty-one eyebars at an angle to protrude from the structure and grasp the cable strands. And, finally, pour the concrete, heroic amounts, to create anchorages weighing 270 million pounds each, capable of supporting cables sustaining roadway and traffic. So too did the land-based pier for the north tower offer a straightforward construction challenge: Clear and level the foundation; build a cofferdam of steel sheet piling; crisscross its interior with a maze of reinforcing steel bars; fill the interior with 23,500 cubic yards of concrete. The approach spans and the soaring arch over Fort Point were equally straightforward, utilizing, as they did, state-of-the-art but standard bridge-building techniques already in use. Still, the arch over Fort Point possessed a grandeur all its own, especially when viewed from below; for it constituted a kind of overture, a prelude to the epic, a bridge within a bridge, its classical design, an arch over land, Roman in simplicity, recalling the basic vocabulary of ancient engineering.

The south pier site, by contrast, presented a challenge of unprecedented complexity. It was, for one thing, 1,125 feet offshore, its bedrock having caused such controversy during the planning process. Tides ran from between five and seven knots in velocity, bringing along alluvial debris that made the water inky black. Operating from a barge, deep-sea divers reconnoitered the strait floor in search of sites where wells could be dynamited to anchor the pier foundation to bedrock. Because of the pressure involved, divers could rarely spend more than twenty minutes at one hundred feet, literally working in the dark, before being brought to the surface at a slow but steady rate to avoid the bends. Once foundation anchorage points had been located and blasted to an appropriate depth and a fender built around the site, plans called for the sinking of a caisson to the floor of the strait, then pumping it clear to create the necessary space. One foggy morning, however, a ship rammed into the floating caisson, damaging it beyond repair. Towed out to sea, the caisson was sunk, and Plan B went into operation. An 1,125-foot working trestle was built out from the shore, and a steel and concrete fender was built up from the bottom of the strait. Pumped clear of water, the oval-shaped fender created an open space 300 feet long and 155 feet wide, the size of a football field. In this space wrestled temporarily from the sea, a framework was constructed of concrete honeycombed with rods of reinforcing steel. Pour 130,000 cubic yards of concrete. Let it dry. A completed pier now rose 110 feet below mean low water level, 44 feet above the surface, surrounded by a fender 100 feet below mean low water level and 15 feet above the surface. Once the concrete had dried, strip away the framework and reflood the space between the pier and the fender. Polish the surface of the pier.

Next came the towers. Rising 746 feet above the waters of the strait, these two structures were taller, by 190 feet, than the Washington Monument and ranked alongside the tallest skyscrapers of New York City. Each tower consisted of two parallel legs, set 90 feet apart at the outer leg, joined at six intervals by struts or crossbraces, four of which, above the roadway, were sheathed in decorative casing. Each tower leg rested upon a foundation of thick steel plating, which in turn rested upon the top surface of the concrete pier leveled and ground down to an accuracy within $1/32$ of an inch. As they rose, the towers tapered, from 33 by 54 feet at their base to 11 by 25 feet at their height. Each tower was constructed of hollow steel cells, silicon steel on the outer sections, carbon steel in the interior, $3^1/2$ feet square, riveted one to another at a decreasing rate, from ninety-seven cells at the base of each tower leg to twenty-one cells at the summit. The boom or arm of a traveler or creeper derrick located atop each pier in the center roadway space lifted each cell from a barge below and swung it into place, where it was attached with rivets heated on the site in waist-high, coal-burning forges resembling barbecues. Fifteen times, when the cells reached a certain height, the derrick and the riveters' scaffolding were lifted to higher positions within each tower until the summit was reached. Altogether, 404 cells, averaging 45 tons each, were riveted together (600,000 rivets in each tower), forming two skyscraper-high honeycombs, through the interior spaces of which ran twenty-three miles of ladders and one elevator leading to the summit. Atop each leg of each tower were placed 150-ton saddles, four in all, on which the Bridge cables, once spun, would rest. The saddle casings that received the cables rested on steel rollers allowing for up to $5^1/2$ feet of adjustment, depending upon load. The decorative casings and corner brackets designed by Irving Morrow, meanwhile, were lifted into place and riveted, and by June 28, 1935, 104 days ahead of schedule, the two towers rose triumphantly from their sites: at once self-referencing—ends in themselves, Art Deco constructions of beauty and power, Eiffel Towers—but promising as well, in no uncertain terms, the Bridge to come.

It would be a Bridge whose roadway would be suspended from two cables rising and descending in a graceful reverse arch across 7,650 feet of defined and enhanced space. Cables as powerful as these, capable of supporting 400 million pounds of weight, are too heavy to be constructed on land and lifted into place. They must, rather, be assembled on-site, in the sky, atop their towers where they will do their work, through a process of spinning spliced wire into strands and compacting these strands into cables. For the two transverse cables of the Golden Gate Bridge, 80,000 miles of spliced wire 0.196 inches in diameter—smaller than the diameter of a lead pencil but with a breaking strength of 7,000 pounds—were spun across the 7,650 feet between anchorages via four three-wheel spinning machines suspended from overhead cables. At mid-point, at the lowest level of suspension, wheels were exchanged from carriage to carriage (each carriage made the trip halfway before returning) so as to allow for continuous spinning. Traveling at 640 feet per minute, these spinning wheels were capable of laying down an average of 173 tons of wire each working day.

At critical points across the distance, workers banded an average of 452 wires into hexagonal strands. After being brought into alignment, these strands were laid side by side and upon each other into a hexagonal assembly. When sixty-one strands were assembled, six circular hydraulic jacks—compacting machines consisting of twelve radial hydraulics rams, each of them capable of exerting pressures of 6,000 pounds per square inch for a total of 972 tons of pressure—moved along each collection of strands and compressed them into a single cable bound in cast-iron bands and clamps. The cable was then encased in its entirety in a sheath of tightly wound galvanized wire that created a flexible yet protective outer surface. Each completed cable, 36⅜ inches in diameter, was under 63 million pounds of pull or tension from its own weight as, defying gravity, it rose and reverse-arched toward the anchorages on either shore. At the anchorages, the cables splayed into strands, which distributed the load as each strand looped around strand shoes affixed to the ends of eyebars, which were in turn attached to other eyebars fixed to the foundation and embedded in the concrete.

Once the cables were in place, 250 pairs of vertical steel ropes, 2¹¹⁄₁₆ inches in diameter, were attached to steel casings bolted around the cables and dropped to a uniform length to support the steel roadway framework. Built out from each tower toward the center in corresponding increments to equalize weight on the cables, the steel components of the roadway were lifted into place by derricks from land or from barges, large beams first, then smaller stringers. Throughout the last months of 1935 until the end of 1936, the roadway framework crept its way across the strait. Just as the towers, when standing alone, were possessed, if only momentarily, of their own coherent beauty and meaning, the sections of roadway advancing toward each other across the strait—like the two sections of railway advancing across the continent in the last century—emanated a drama of their own, of technology in motion, struggling toward its final form, and the brave new future technology would create. On November 18, 1936, the roadways were joined at the center of the strait; and, from a distance at least, the Golden Gate Bridge stood complete in definition and grandeur.

Because the roadway was designed to withstand a downward deflection of eleven feet and an upward thrust of six, the concrete roadbed had to be poured as adjacent sections allowing the roadway to bend if necessary with its supporting structure. Prior to the pouring of the concrete sections, wooden frameworks were constructed on the underside of the steel roadway structure, and a network of reinforcing crossbars established. Once the concrete was poured and dried, the roadway was paved with asphalt, the final step in integrating the Bridge into the California State Highway system.

On the Marin side, the Division of Highways was busy on the Waldo project: the highway and tunnel leading onto the Bridge, together with an ancillary road curving downward into Sausalito. On the San Francisco side, the District bore responsibility, along with other relevant agencies, for the construction of a two-pronged access: a direct approach by viaduct from the Marina district to the east, subsequently named in honor of Frank Doyle, the Santa Rosa banker, and a connection via tunnel on Park Presidio Boulevard running south. Originally, two toll plazas had been planned, but the decision was made to collect tolls only on the southern side, partially for reasons of economy but also because the northern approach had already been paid for by public funds and was not part of the bond redemption scheme. For the southern toll plaza, Strauss wanted a grand entrance, something resembling the Arc de Triomphe. Budget considerations, however, made that impossible, and for the toll plaza Irving Morrow designed a serviceable row of rounded and streamlined steel and glass toll booths in a style fusing Art Deco and Moderne.

Such a titanic job of construction required first-rate management, and in such figures as Cone, Reed, Paine, and others, the construction of the Golden Gate Bridge received exactly that. But an army cannot consist of officers alone, however talented; and a great bridge—while it owes so much to its designers and construction supervisors—owes an equal, if not superior, debt of gratitude to the workers who built it. Part of Russ Cone's charisma as supervising engineer was the fact that he embodied the engineer as avatar of the recovery of the American economy from the thralldom of the Great Depression. And so too did each and every worker on the Golden Gate Bridge project embody, if more collectively, the possibility, indeed the probability, that the American economy was not finished, nor was the American worker down for the count.

Reprised today through photographs and, in some cases, through oral histories and interviews they gave in old age, the construction workers on the Golden Gate Bridge—divers, ironworkers, riveters, barge and derrick operators, cable spinners, carpenters, pourers of concrete, scaffolding and ladder men, painters aloft in their bosun's chairs, each of them wearing the leather safety helmets Strauss required on the job, their overalls spattered with concrete or paint, their weathered faces frequently showing fatigue by the end of a workday, along with stubble and five o'clock shadows; or photographed at noon, sitting on top of the world, lunch pails in their laps; or taking a mid-morning break, a cigarette dangling from their lips—survive in photographs as a Depression-era documentary of men glad for a job, willing to risk the high steel, at a time when millions of Americans were out of work.

Photographs reveal no women on-site, no Rosie the Riveter in this pre–World War II era, with the exception of timekeepers or other office help or lunchroom attendants on Fort Point. No black or Asian faces emerge in surviving photographs: painful to acknowledge, but even more painful, at the time, for the men who were being denied hiring or the required admission to unions because of race. It was a racially restricted time for the construction trades—indeed, for the entire nation—and would remain so into the second half of World War II, and even then progress would be minimal.

Each generation, however, lives in its own time and reflects the strengths and deficiencies of an era. The working men of the 1930s lived at a time of discrimination, true; but they also lived at a time in which personal physical effort, hands-on labor, still defined the tasks performed by the majority of American workers. Nowhere was this more the case than in bridge construction. For all its technological feats and intricacies, for all the barges and derricks, jackhammers and spinning wheels involved, each function, each job on the Golden Gate Bridge required a direct application of human effort at every level—hands, muscles, balance, eyesight, brainpower, and survival smarts. Each and every task demanded physical effort and concentration of the most intense sort, both for the sake of the task at hand and for personal survival.

The Golden Gate Bridge might very well be an engineering concept of Pythagorean beauty, designed by a panel of experts and at least one near-genius. But it was also a monumental struggle to fabricate steel in distant places, to ship it from one side of the country to the other and rivet it into position, to pour untold tons of concrete and spin wire into cables more than seven hundred feet above the surging sea. Everything was so extrordinary, so unprecedented, so dangerous. The construction of the anchorages involved the removal of 3.25 million cubic feet of earth and pouring of concrete into frameworks twelve stories high, the equivalent of building two skyscrapers. Even this task, seemingly so simple—the distribution of concrete through a long tube called the elephant trunk—demanded a special level of skill, given the tendency of the wet concrete to create air pockets, which, if not corrected, could provide dangerous flaws in the final structures, hampering their ability to secure 63 million pounds of pull with the precision of adjustable machinery.

Ordinary workers soon learned to perform at an extraordinary level. Some of them were experienced iron-workers, electricians, carpenters, and other contracting trades, and they tended to receive the higher wages, up to eleven dollars per day. But others were new recruits to the field, some of them claiming prior experience they did not have and even more faking local addresses so as to benefit from the preference given to local workers. And always, as they worked, they were aware of the daily gathering of 100 to 150 men at the foot of the bridge at Fort Baker, hanging around, waiting for someone to get fired or hurt so that they might be called up by the Ironworkers Union, Local 377, which did the hiring.

Recruitment for undersea work was another matter, for no eager beaver, however willing, could master the skills of undersea site clearance and foundation preparation in tides that, twice a day, emptied one sixth of San Francisco Bay into the Pacific, three and a half times the volume of water flowing from the Mississippi into the Gulf of Mexico. Nothing like this had ever been tried before: the creation of a cleared and dry space the size of a football field in the midst of such a torrent, freezing cold, at depths allowing for, on the average, no more than four twenty-minute sessions of work per day. And so experts were called in: men such as Johnny Bacon, Bob Patching, and Chris Hansen, veteran divers with national reputations, who not only dynamited the wells for the south pier but, following that, cleared the site of debris with high-pressure underwater hoses capable of overcoming the torrential tides. If clearing the site was not enough, inspection wells were driven even farther into the rock, down another ten feet or so, allowing chief consulting geologist Andrew Lawson to descend into the very core of the disputed site, once it was pumped clear, and with his geologist's hammer bang on the rock walls, proclaiming the serpentine stone as strong as the steel being shipped from Pennsylvania.

Working that steel—unloading it from barges, lifting it into position, riveting it into place—was the prerogative of the unionized ironworkers, the core of them professionals,

During the construction of the Bridge, workers built a catwalk that connected the towers at both sides of the strait so that they could spin cables for the Bridge. Photo taken September 20, 1935. (© *Bettmann/CORBIS*)

with experience on the bridges and skyscrapers of the nation, but novice ironworkers were present as well, getting used to the winds, the cold, the heights, and in one case, an earthquake .6 in magnitude that had workers clinging to swaying steel as they upchucked their latest meal from motion sickness. At open heights such as this—five, six hundred feet above the water, facing strong winds coming in from an open sea—temperatures could drop as much as thirty degrees on a given day. Risking their dexterity, men wore overcoats or double, even triple layers of sweaters. In the summer, fog banks compounded the cold and obscured vision, which was a frightening thing, given the fact that at all times the Bridge site was an orchestration of dangerous objects in constant movement: steel being swung into place; tools and construction materials being accidentally dropped; superheated rivets being heated aloft on precariously perched forges, then funneled through tubes to riveters working in near darkness inside the steel cells, or, if outside, tossed from forge to riveter through the air and caught with handheld funnels. During the cable-spinning process, the spinning carriages moved from tower to tower at rapid speed above a catwalk. Get hit by a cable carriage, when distracted, or by flying objects of any sort, and you were in trouble. The only fatality in the project, up to the final days, came from such an accident, when Kermit Moore, a twenty-three-year-old San Franciscan employed by Bethlehem Steel, was crushed to death by a toppling derrick. Another less immediate but more insidious danger was that of lead poisoning from primer or other leads released into the atmosphere by heat or friction and inhaled. For a time, until the problem was tackled head-on by an avoidance of lead-based primer and mandatory breathing masks for riveters and other exposed workers, the infirmary had a steady population of lead-poisoning victims, some of them damaged for life.

All things considered, it was a demanding, dangerous, but not a grinding culture as far as workers were concerned. Cost controls were always in effect. A worker's time sheet did not begin until he reached his actual work site, even if that meant a thirty- to forty-minute climb up a tower. Show any sign of incompetence and you were off the job, easy to replace, even in a union environment. The Roebling Company, however, surprised its workers with a very enlightened policy: If you were not busy at any one time, don't sweat it, don't fake work, relax, take a cigarette break. By its very definition, cable spinning involved rhythms of intensity and release, busyness and time spent waiting for the next task. Makework, looking busy, could screw up the process.

Strauss himself was very much concerned for workers' safety. A rule of thumb in bridge construction was one death for every one million dollars spent. Strauss vowed to beat

Construction on the catwalk that supported men and equipment five hundred feet above the waters of the Bay. The safety-minded Joseph Strauss built a safety net under the Bridge at a cost of $130,000, but ten men fell to their deaths on February 17, 1937, when a platform collapsed and the net gave way. (© Underwood & Underwood/CORBIS)

the odds. He established the hard-hat requirement, soon to become a standard throughout the construction industry. On Monday mornings, he provided free sauerkraut juice for workers suffering from hangovers. Most dramatically, he spent a considerable sum, more than $130,000, on a safety net, a web of six-inch squares woven from manila rope, cantilevered and suspended beneath the roadway. Ten feet wider than the Bridge, the innovative net provided a sense of safety and security; hence it increased productivity. A total of nineteen men fell into it and survived to become members of the elite Halfway to Hell Club. So confident were workers in the net, Russ Cone threatened to fire anyone who dove into it just to show off.

As the Bridge neared completion, it looked like Strauss might have beaten the odds. The Bridge was budgeted at $35 million, including administrative costs, but only one life had been lost. As the laying of the roadway began its final stages—the dismantling of the wooden frame from a traveling platform beneath the roadway, then passing its plywood and two-by-fours piece by piece upward through

The Bridge with cables nearing completion, as seen from the Marin side. *(© Underwood & Underwood/CORBIS)*

a bucket brigade—luck ran out. The traveling platform was secured to the roadway by bolts. Already, on the first day of the stripping process, before the platform was even put in use, workers complained that these bolts were too short to insure a proper grip, "too goddam short" as one worker put it. A safety inspector was en route to the platform on the morning of February 17, 1937, when an horrendous staccato sound, like machine-gun fire, shook the Bridge. The five-ton stripping platform beneath the north tower was breaking loose from its moorings and was dragging down the safety net. Twelve workers were thrown into the abyss, some of them clinging to the ripped net and trying to climb it like a ladder to safety. A photographer on the south shore captured the horror of their descent. Two men survived the fall, ironworker Evan (Slim) Lambert, twenty-seven, foreman of the stripping crew, miraculously unscathed, and Oscar Osberg, a fifty-one-year-old carpenter who was pulled from the water with a fractured hip, a broken leg, and serious internal injuries. Although Fred Dummatzen, twenty-four, survived the fall, he was hit by falling debris and died of hypothermia and injuries as Slim Lambert tried to swim him to shore. Nine men either died on impact or became enmeshed in the net and were drowned. Two other workers grabbed onto girders just as the stripping platform began to tilt. One of them, Tom Casey, hung on for several minutes before being rescued, his pipe still clenched tight between his teeth. A coroner's jury found the bolts at fault, as did the state Industrial Accident Commission. Strauss and Paine openly attributed guilt to Pacific Bridge, which in turn blamed a lack of supervision by Strauss, Paine, Cone, and others down the line. No charges were ever filed.

-9-

CITY

As a city-based structure, the Golden Gate Bridge serves and enhances the urban identity of San Francisco. The very naming of the strait and entrance as Chrysopylae by John Charles Frémont in 1846 in reference to the Golden Horn of Constantinople prophetically linked the channel entrance to the not-yet-built metropolis that would inevitably arise on the shores of San Francisco Bay. Not only was Frémont's implied prediction realized, the Golden Horn/Constantinople comparison affixed itself to the San Francisco identity as a recurrent metaphor. Even when it was still but a ramshackle town on the empty edge of a half-settled continent, San Francisco knew itself as a city destined for civic grandeur and commercial vitality. As early as 1855, still in frontier status, San Francisco produced an eight-hundred-page history of itself, *The Annals of San Francisco*, chronicling the foundations of an overnight maritime colony destined for bigger things. In the decades that followed, starting as early as the *Annals* themselves, proposal after proposal to bridge San Francisco Bay were anchored in and energized by the knowledge that for San Francisco to achieve its destined identity as a great city it had to escape its water-bound peninsula and make connections with its hinterlands beyond ferry service. In time, that railroad and horse-drawn connection developed into an electric interurban connection as well and, finally and most powerfully by the third decade of the twentieth century, a direct connection by automobile. Since ancient times, cities have required their hinterlands for social, economic, and cultural development; and the hinterlands, in turn, took their identity from the city, the oldest and most sophisticated of political institutions beyond the tribal, whether Sumer, Babylon, Jerusalem, Athens, Rome, or Constantinople.

Such perennial ambitions were on the minds of the city planners and builders of the Renaissance and Baroque as, starting with the rebuilding of Rome between 1585 and 1590 by Pope Sixtus V, they sought to recapture the forums, squares, plazas, fountains, staircases, obelisks and columns, boulevards, bridges, and open spaces of the classical city, imposing such features across the following centuries on the previously huddled medieval densities of Rome, Paris, London, Berlin, and Vienna. Madrid, a new city, was fashioned from the beginning according to these norms. Through the Laws of the Indies, they were translated in the 1570s to the newly developing Spanish colonial cities of the New World. In the 1790s this dream of neo-classical grandeur arrived in the newly founded Republic of the United States of America via Major Pierre L'Enfant's plan for Washington, D.C. One hundred years later, this effort to impose order on otherwise spontaneous urban places animated the City Beautiful movement, beginning with Daniel Hudson Burnham's plans for Chicago.

In 1905 Burnham created a City Beautiful Plan for San Francisco. Although it was not fully implemented in the aftermath of the destruction of the city in April 1906, as many thought it should be, the Burnham Plan exercised its influence over the rebuilding of San Francisco, as evident in the neo-classical grandeur of the newly constructed Civic Center, the Great Highway on the western edge of the city, the tunnels through Twin Peaks, on Stockton and Irving streets, and the maintenance or widening of Geary, Van Ness, and Lombard into boulevards, together with continuing calls for the development of a St. Peter's–like colonnade and plaza in front of the Ferry Building, and other

City Beautiful amenities, whether realized or—in the case of the Ferry Building Plaza, the extension of the Golden Gate Park Panhandle into the Civic Center, or the development of an Acropolis of fountains, stairways, and plazas atop Twin Peaks—merely hanging on in memory and hope.

The contours of these City Beautiful dreams, in all their texture and color and architectural appeal, survive most obviously in the Burnham Plan as filed with the San Francisco Board of Supervisors on April 17, 1906, a day before earthquake and fire destroyed the city. These proposals can also be recovered in the sketches and publications of the post-earthquake Philopolis (Friend of the City) movement centered on the husband-and-wife artistic team of Arthur and Lucia Mathews, dedicated to advancing Arts and Crafts and City Beautiful values in the rebuilding of San Francisco. Arthur and Lucia had spent time as art students in Paris, Arthur at the Académie Julian in the late 1880s, Lucia at the Académie Carmen a decade later. Married since 1894, the couple maintained a workshop and studio on California Street from which emanated an array of paintings, furniture, and hand-crafted and hand-painted objets d'art that put the Mathewses in the forefront of the Decorative Style that represented the California version of the Arts and Crafts movement. Following the 1906 earthquake and fire, the Mathewses founded *Philopolis* magazine, promoting the aesthetic challenges facing San Francisco as it rebuilt itself. In Paris Arthur Mathews had closely studied the renowned French muralist Puvis de Chavannes, and it was as a muralist, as well as a painter strongly inspired by James McNeill Whistler, that Arthur Mathews was destined to make his most enduring contribution to American art.

In 1913 Mathews received a commission from the California state legislature to do an ambitious mural for the state capitol in Sacramento depicting the history of California. To this task, Mathews brought his full powers as a Romantic neo-classicist colorist in the style of Puvis de Chavannes. Completed in 1914, the fourth and final panel of the mural, *The City*, depicted the rise of a modernized Constantinople-like city on the shores of an azure bay—in short, an idealized San Francisco. Here, indeed, was artistic and architectural San Francisco's deepest dream of itself as far as the City Beautiful movement was concerned: an orchestration of domed and colonnaded buildings, including stylized high-rises, connected by boulevards planted in laurel, eucalyptus, Monterey cypress, and pine, set against a sea and sky alive with color. This same vision of San Francisco as Constantinople reborn, the City Beautiful, pervaded the Panama-Pacific International Exposition under construction on the shores of the Bay as Mathews painted his murals in Sacramento; indeed, in so many ways—most dramatically in the domed and colonnaded Palace of Fine

Arts, preserved as a civic monument following the dismantlement of the Exposition—the Panama-Pacific International Exposition represented in festival architecture a compensatory daydream of San Francisco as City Beautiful on the part of a real-life city that had been forced to rebuild itself as quickly as possible.

From this perspective, the Golden Gate Bridge—by 1930, that is, after its initial redesign—was also a product of the same imaginative and emotional impulse. The initial design for the Golden Gate Bridge constituted an affront to the City Beautiful impulse that continued to reverberate so powerfully within the collective imagination of architectural and artistic San Francisco, then in the process of rebuilding the city, if not according to the literal demands of the City Beautiful movement, then at the least in a spirit of distinguished Beaux-Arts and Mediterranean Revival architecture that would by mid-century make of San Francisco one of the most attractive cities in the nation.

Not only did engineers Leon Moisseiff and Charles Alton Ellis make the Golden Gate Bridge higher, lighter, stronger, and longer in span, they also made it more beautiful via a straightforward presentation of structural elements running parallel through the best of classical design. Architect Irving Morrow, in turn—a man fully aware of the City Beautiful and Philopolis movements, a year-long visitor to the Panama-Pacific International Exposition—had sufficient genius to harmonize, indeed to discipline, the exuberant runaway possibilities of Art Deco with a restraint thoroughly classical in inspiration. Thus the Golden Gate Bridge, as an urban construct animated by City Beautiful ideals, swept forth from the city as a grand boulevard held aloft by sculpted towers in full view of a panorama of sea, sky, and city—the Piranesean dome of the Palace of Fine Arts; the Mediterranean Revival villas of the Marina district in all their pastel color; the laurels, Monterey cypresses, and pines of the Presidio and Lands End; the herons, egrets, pelicans, and seagulls flecking blue sky with whiteness—that Arthur Mathews himself had done his best to evoke in mural for the state capitol. The Bridge, in short, was urban in its founding impulse and City Beautiful in its architectural statement. In linking San Francisco to the empty headlands of Marin, moreover, the Golden Gate Bridge was underscoring the very nature of California itself, at once urbanized and environmentally inspiring.

While the designers of the Golden Gate Bridge, in contrast to the San Francisco–Oakland Bay Bridge, had resisted rail transit, more than adequate provisions for pedestrian traffic had been provided. From the very date it was opened, May 27, 1937, the Bridge welcomed pedestrians, a full day before it welcomed automobiles. For pedestrians, the Bridge provided the grandest of promenades, and even after it was opened to vehicular traffic the following morning it continued to provide one of the most popular promenades in the nation. Indeed, those who first walked across the Bridge that day in late May 1937, an estimated two hundred thousand of them, realized they were doing something historic and hence sought, many of them, to be the first this or the first that, however ridiculous—the first twins, the first man on stilts, the first person to walk across backward, the first to roller-skate, the first to tap-dance across, the first to cross barefoot—in a folkloric effort to establish a record, however eccentric, that might prove of lasting value. The majority of pedestrians that opening day tended to be dressed in their Sunday best, leading children by the hand or pushing babies in carriages, as if out for a Sunday stroll in Golden Gate Park, enjoying the pleasures of seeing and being seen in public places that are among the special pleasures of city life.

For them and for the millions of visitors to come, the Bridge afforded an opportunity for urban recreation. It opened with the nine-day Golden Gate Bridge Fiesta, running from May 25 to June 2, 1937, through a gamut of activities: an historical outdoor pageant on Crissy Field involving the efforts of three thousand costumed participants, a show featuring prominent radio stars, an internationally themed civic luncheon, a grand Fiesta Ball, all this in the Civic Auditorium. There was, of course, the Pedes-

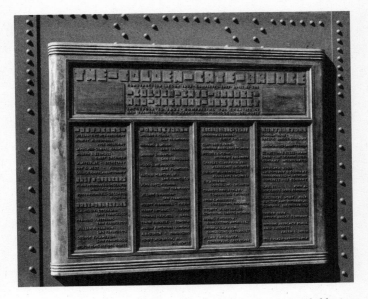

The dedication plaque of the Golden Gate Bridge, as unmistakably Art Deco as the Bridge itself. The Golden Gate Bridge was opened on May 27, 1937, marked by a twelve-hour pedestrian walk with an estimated two hundred thousand participants. *(Library of Congress)*

trian Walk itself, running from 6:00 A.M. to 6:00 P.M. on Thursday the twenty-seventh, starting off with a grand parade to Crissy Field, and that evening, after the Bridge had closed and the sun set, a pageant starring the opera singer John Charles Thomas followed by fireworks. On Friday, May 28, came the opening of the Bridge to automobile traffic, kicked off by a massive flight of military aircraft and a cavalcade of historic automobiles. That afternoon at 3:00 P.M. a considerable portion of the U.S. Fleet—more than a hundred vessels manned by sixty thousand officers and men, fresh from Pacific maneuvers—sailed under the Bridge while flights of naval airplanes flew overhead. There were more fireworks that evening, and the ships of the fleet, now at anchor in the Bay, were illuminated. An equestrian demonstration by Army cavalry units, wrestling matches in the Civic Auditorium, and a concert in Sigmund Stern Grove rounded out the day.

Saturday the twenty-ninth saw the Fiesta shift to Marin with yacht races and athletic contests, followed that evening by more fireworks and a grand ball. Sunday the thirtieth began with special services in the churches of the city and Marin, followed by memorial services for the Bridge workers who had lost their lives and, on a happier note, a mammoth parade of yachts on the Bay. On Monday the thirty-first, Memorial Day, there was a military parade at noon followed by an Army versus Navy baseball game and a concert by massed military bands in Civic Auditorium that evening. Tuesday, June 1, saw more children-oriented events in the morning, followed that evening by a civic dinner in honor of the warrant officers of the Fleet and a ball for enlisted men in the Civic Auditorium. Wednesday the second ended the Fiesta with a military and naval ball for officers and invited dignitaries.

Opening in 1939, the Golden Gate International Exposition on Treasure Island celebrated the completion of the San

Francisco–Oakland Bay and Golden Gate bridges, together with the creation of the exposition site, Treasure Island, through a massive dredging and filling of shoals adjacent to Yerba Buena Island. Running from February to October 1939, then reorganized for a second run from May to September 1940, the Golden Gate International Exposition was themed—as was evident in Ralph Stackpole's eighty-foot-high statue *Pacifica*—to the emergence of the Bay Area as a hub of a developing Asia/Pacific Basin trade and culture zone embracing East and Southeast Asia, Australia, New Zealand, the Pacific islands, and the Pacific coasts of North and South America, whose vital futurism was embodied in each of the great bridges just completed. When the seaborne Panama Clipper passenger plane, en route to Manila, taxied down the waters of a lagoon adjacent to the San Francisco–Oakland Bay Bridge, took gracefully to the air, then flew over the Golden Gate Bridge, heading for Honolulu, it was most easy to believe, or at least to have hope, that an era of peace, prosperity, and technological progress would soon be transforming the Asia/Pacific Basin into the Mediterranean of modern times. Alas, Pearl Harbor ended such hopes, and the Navy claimed Treasure Island for a base. The heroic statue *Pacifica* was dismantled as the United States joined the bitter war even then raging throughout the Pacific.

Still, a celebratory, recreational meaning had been attached to the two bridges, and when Congress in 1972 established the Golden Gate National Recreation Area (GGNRA) in San Francisco and Marin counties, the scene was set for a more permanent and glorious development of the Golden Gate Bridge as site and symbol of urban enjoyment. In time, Crissy Field at the base of the Bridge, now part of the GGNRA, was decommissioned, its military airstrip removed, and the site returned to its natural condition of seashore, inlets, and lagoons. A Bayside promenade was created between the St. Francis Yacht Club and Fort Point, spectacular in its view of the city, the Bay and its islands, the green hills of the Presidio, the Golden Gate Bridge, the channel itself, leading out to the ocean, and the headlands of Marin. Each day, on weekends especially, thousands of Bay Area residents flock to Crissy Field to walk or cycle along the shore to and from the Bridge, to picnic or fish from pier or shore, or, attired in wetsuits, to launch themselves on surfboards, windsurfers, or kite-sailers into the choppy waters of the Bay. Thus the GGNRA in general and the Golden Gate Promenade on Crissy Field in particular had become by the early twenty-first century one of the most engaging urban recreational sites in the nation, made even more compelling by the great Bridge ever in view.

Urban as well is the fact that the Golden Gate Bridge, Highway, and Transportation District, as it was renamed in 1971, retained its autonomy as an independent agency. Over the years there have been numerous attempts to absorb the

District into the state Division of Highways or one or another super-agency. This effort became especially intense in the late 1950s and early 1960s when the business sector, allied with elected officials hostile to the independent authority of the District, pushed for a Bay Area–wide Golden Gate Authority responsible for planning and transportation throughout the entire region. Animated by a post-war planning philosophy of consolidation—with its emphasis on regional solutions and enforcement—supporters of the proposed Golden Gate Authority argued that only a mega-agency, structured as a pro-growth, public/private cooperative, could handle the planning and transportation challenges facing a rapidly growing Bay Area. At the time, modernist solutions such as this, emphasizing efficiency over local control, seemed inevitable. Animated by a philosophy and practice of localism and enlightened self-interest, the Bridge District directors resisted what for a while seemed to be an almost foregone consolidation of power and authority, just as they had previously resisted various efforts by the state to absorb the District into the Division of Highways or otherwise submit it to state control.

Modernist planners and the leaders of the great Bay Area corporations considered the Bridge District an anachronism from the Progressive Era: a self-perpetuating board of non-elected directors, that is, exempted from public scrutiny or removal, primarily loyal not to voters—commuters from Marin County, for example, who paid the bulk of the tolls—or to elected officials, but to the Golden Gate Bridge itself and, most obviously, their own status as directors. The directors, in short, were running a municipal-type government without the obligation to run for office. Like any surviving city politicians, moreover, the directors of the Bridge were adept at the blood sport of city politics, beating back effort after effort to usurp their authority. Like any effective city government, the directors quickly realized that a safely deceased Founder would strengthen civic identity, hence help beat back reccurring attempts at takeover. Joseph Strauss died of a heart attack in Los Angeles on May 18, 1938. In May 1941 the directors dedicated a life-size bronze statue of Strauss mounted on a raised pedestal at the San Francisco entrance, fully worthy of the controversial figure now accepted as beloved Founder since he was no longer a troublesome impresario to be managed. In time, like any civic oligarchy, the directors would nurture and enlarge Strauss's status as prophetic visionary to the total detriment of acknowledging the contribution of others. A city called the Golden Gate Bridge District, in short, now had its mythic Founder, safely at rest.

Like any city officials anxious to stay in office, the District directors operated at a reasonable level of stewardship over the next three decades. Historians have chronicled their shortcomings, even their outright failures. On February 9,

1938, for example, winds approaching eighty miles per hour deflected the center of the Bridge by ten feet from its normal position and created a wavelike undulation of up to thirty vibrations per minute. Bridge engineer Russell Cone submitted a confidential report alerting the directors to possible long-term problems, which the directors—advised by Clifford Paine, who had succeeded Strauss as trusted consultant—ignored, indeed suppressed from public knowledge. Then, on November 7, 1940, the Tacoma Narrows Bridge in Washington state, also designed by Leon Moisseiff, buffeted by similar winds, collapsed completely, a mere four months after its opening. Clifford Paine said not to worry, and the directors agreed.

Ignoring the Cone report on the February 1938 storm and the implications of the Tacoma Narrows collapse constituted a serious misjudgment, no doubt about it; but the all-clear given by Paine, the continuation of the Depression through 1941, and the Second World War can be entered into mitigation. On December 1, 1951, however, yet another violent windstorm—with gusting winds reaching up to sixty-nine miles per hour—swept through the channel, closing the Bridge for three hours during rush hour, the first such closing in its history. Once again, the directors went into denial; but this time Clifford Paine, called in once more to consult, had some very bad news. During the height of the storm, Paine reported, the center span had undulated some ten feet ten inches and swayed sideways in either direction in about the same amount. A number of vertical suspenders had been torn loose from their sleeves at deck level. The entire Bridge, moreover, now stood an inch and a half out of line. Had the storm lasted another half hour, Paine concluded, the Bridge might very well have collapsed. Shaken, the directors appropriated $3 million to reinforce and stiffen the roadway with 250 steel struts, which increased the torsional rigidity of the Bridge by a factor of thirty-five. Completed in the fall of 1954, the project cost two men their lives when, in a horrible replay of February 1937, a scaffold broke from its moorings and fell into the sea.

Critics of the directors frequently leveled charges of corruption. Yet while the occasional padding of expense accounts, the wining and dining of political and associational allies, and the large sums spent on public relations and advertising can be held in negative balance, along with the failure of the District to hire minorities until forced to do so by civil rights legislation, no major scandal—no egregious instance of graft or malfeasance, no indictments—ever surfaced, just a continual roller coaster of political infighting characteristic of local politics. The faults and infractions that can be leveled against the Bridge District directors, moreover, can also be seen in the context of American public practice in the 1930–65 era, with its more casual approach to perks and prerogatives, along with the de facto discrimination remaining in effect across the nation.

And besides: not only in the Bay Area but throughout the United States, government was heading in a different direction. By the year 2002 special districts such as the Golden Gate Bridge, Highway, and Transportation District constituted 40 percent of all local governments throughout the nation. Americans were increasingly preferring to deal with their public business on a local or regional basis through a genre, the independent district, that the Golden Gate Bridge District had helped to pioneer. The San Francisco Bay Area itself, meanwhile, as well as greater Los Angeles, had resisted uniting as a metropolitan authority by means of super-agencies or, when such region-wide agencies were necessary—as in the case, say, of air quality control—conferring on such agencies the high degree of autonomy enjoyed by the Golden Gate Bridge, Highway, and Transportation District.

Thus when the newly funded (1962) Bay Area Rapid Transit District (BART), whose directors were elected, pushed for the construction of a second level on the Golden Gate Bridge, so as to run BART trains north to Santa Rosa, the non-elected directors of the Bridge District, as might be expected, resisted, and so did the environmentally oriented sector of Marin County voters, previously so critical of the Bridge District, fearful that BART service would usher into Marin and Sonoma counties an era of runaway growth. Indeed, the first BART plan envisioned the entire Bay Area unified into one ultra-modernist rapid transit network. As it turned out, Sonoma, Marin, Napa, San Mateo, and Santa Clara counties opted out of the BART program: which constituted, for better or for worse, a dramatic rejection of modernist planning.

BART never ran across a lower second tier on the Golden Gate Bridge. Instead, the District got into the bus and ferry business. The impetus behind BART—to reduce automotive traffic throughout the Bay Area—was nowhere more evident than on the Highway 101 corridor crossing the Golden Gate Bridge. First of all, the Bridge as an urban function had played a crucial role in the development of the North Bay hinterlands. That, after all, had been among the two or three most compelling reasons for the construction of the Bridge in the first place—why even Del Norte County on the Oregon border joined the District—to bring growth and development to the Redwood Empire. Indeed, from the beginning the relationship between the Bridge District and the Redwood Empire was close and continuous. If the District was the city, then the Redwood Empire was the hinterlands: developed first as a resort destination, as the very first annual report of the Golden Gate Bridge and Highway District asserted in 1938, noting how automotive traffic had spiked in the summer

months when the resorts of the Redwood Empire, especially those on the Russian River, were open.

Following the war ensued the suburbanization of southern Marin County and the rise of Santa Rosa as a second
San Francisco, peopled by a mass migration of longtime San
Francisco residents, Irish and Italian Americans especially,
to that Sonoma County town whose leading banker, Frank
Doyle, had played such an important role in the creation
of the District. Thanks to the Bridge as well, Novato in
northern Marin County and Petaluma in southern Sonoma
County emerged as commuter satellites for San Francisco
itself, noticeably popular with policemen, firemen, and
other public servants priced out of the city. Between 1937
and 1967, automotive traffic on the Bridge grew by more
than 750 percent to 28.3 million vehicles annually. There
was even talk of building a second bridge from San Francisco to Tiburon as well as a second level to the Golden
Gate. Less than two years later, the Golden Gate Bridge
was operating at peak capacity, approaching overload during the workweek and on summer weekends. In November
1969 the legislature called for the development of a comprehensive transportation facility plan for the Golden Gate
corridor. Two years later, the legislature intensified and
expanded this mandate.

By that time, the District had already gotten into the
bus business, leasing five coaches from Greyhound. In

September 1971, twenty new coaches were added to a fleet soon to reach 132 buses, and thirty experienced Greyhound drivers were hired. By January 1972, 152 buses were operating from Santa Rosa southward, across the Bridge and into San Francisco. Three high-capacity twenty-five-knot ferries went into operation in 1976 and 1977, financed by federal grants and Bridge revenues. Terminals were built in Sausalito, Larkspur, and San Francisco, and a high-speed catamaran was added to the fleet in 1998. By 2009 five ferries on two routes, Sausalito and Larkspur, were in operation, and some two hundred lift-equipped buses of Golden Gate Bus Transit, with a distinctive red, green, and white logo and color scheme, were carrying more than seven million passengers a year in and out of San Francisco and points in between. Ferry advocates, meanwhile, were envisioning a mid-twenty-first-century ferry culture on San Francisco Bay linking San Jose, Redwood City, and San Francisco in the West Bay; the tri-city Hayward, Newark, and Fremont in the southern East Bay; Oakland, Berkeley, and Martinez to the north, with a possible connection to Sacramento via the Sacramento River; and Sausalito, Tiburon, and Petaluma in the North Bay, with a possible connection to Napa via the Napa River. A pipe dream, perhaps, yet one promulgated by a state commission in a lavish booklet outlining the entire program. District-sponsored ferry service to the Ferry Building in San Francisco helped stimulate the recovery and refurbishment of that long-neglected historic structure into a bustling retail and restaurant emporium, as it had been in times past.

Automobiles, however, remained the Bridge's first constituency. As traffic developed in the post-war era, a number of horrendous fatal crashes by cars drifting into an oncoming lane gave rise to the perpetual question of whether or not a permanent median barrier should be installed. The installation of such a barrier, however, would preclude the alternation of northbound and southbound lanes according to the rhythms of commuter traffic; hence the median question remained a continuing point of contention.

Toll booths represented the primary point of human contact in Bridge operations. Over the years, for millions and millions of crossings—40 million vehicles a year by 2009—contact between driver and uniformed toll-taker has tended to remain routine. Such repetition, of course—with hundreds of cars passing through each toll booth per hour at the height of traffic—involved its own forms of stress for toll-takers. Although the pay and benefits were good, toll-takers were at high risk for burnout, given the highly repetitious and time-charged nature of the task. On the other hand, the paying of a toll to a real live human being humanized the encounter; and because the toll-takers were uniformed, a certain sense of authority was established. An elaborate folklore of unusual encounters eventually grew up, based initially in fact and later embellished as legend. Many reports involved nude or semi-nude female drivers, perhaps a form of wish fulfillment on the part of lonely male toll-takers. One particularly lubricious report, unverified, involved a tryst in the wee hours between a San Francisco go-go dancer and her toll-taker boyfriend. Then there was the escaping bank robber who paid his toll from his cache of loot, or, more cheerful, the gifts offered up, especially during the holiday season: home-made muffins, apple pies, bottles of booze as New Year's Day approached. When tolls were raised—as was frequently the case, with tolls increasing from twenty-five cents to six dollars by September 2008—various forms of commuter hostility surfaced: paying the toll entirely in pennies, for example, thereby forcing a long and tedious recount by the toll-taker; keeping the window on the driver's side uncomfortably closed, thus forcing the toll-taker to negotiate a narrow space in taking money and handing back change; or verbal abuse, excoriating the Bridge, the tolls, the directors, whatever. If a toll could not be paid, toll-takers were authorized to accept valued objects as security, and the roll call of these objects—canes, shoes, fur coats, false teeth—became itself the subject of folkloric embellishment.

Then there was the question of Doyle Drive, the San Francisco entrance to the Bridge. By the early 2000s, after decades of salt air and heavy traffic, the steel understructure of the Doyle Drive viaduct was showing signs of structural degradation. The eastern portion of the drive was located in a potential liquefaction zone that could undermine the entire structure in the case of a serious earthquake. After seven decades, the very design of Doyle Drive seemed substandard. Lane widths were narrow, and there were no medians or shoulders to separate traffic on tight curves or remove stalled vehicles. Nor was there any direct access into the Presidio, a functioning San Francisco district, now that the Army no longer maintained the reserve as its headquarters. In 1991 a Doyle Drive Task Force went to work, and in 1993 it recommended that a new six-lane scenic parkway be built. Over the next decade, the task force of federal, state, and local officials advised by a citizens' committee worked on various solutions, narrowing them down to three alternatives. A final selection for the $1.045 billion project was ready by July 2009, when the shovel-ready design received $50 million in federal stimulus funds and a three-year construction project was announced by Caltrans. The project involved a combination of four at-grade roadways, two tunnels, a low causeway, and a high viaduct sweeping between Crissy Marsh and the Presidio to the toll plaza.

And still, in the midst of all this automobile-oriented

planning for Doyle Drive, the urban-pedestrian culture of the Bridge continued to flourish. The San Francisco–Oakland Bay Bridge had begun its existence with two decks, the lower of them devoted to mass transit; but by April 1958 rail service between San Francisco and Oakland had been discontinued and the lower deck turned into a one-way eastbound crossing. There were no provisions for pedestrians. The Golden Gate Bridge, by contrast, urban from the beginning, welcomed pedestrians and cyclists. By 2009 some ten million pedestrians were crossing the Bridge each year, rendering it a vital component of a tourist economy. The Golden Gate Bridge sustained a city-park intensity of street theater as pedestrians from across the planet crisscrossed it, embraced and kissed, posed for pictures, or, in a number of instances, indulged in political protest: as in the case of a pro-Tibet demonstration during the running of the Olympic Torch across the Bridge in April 2008, in which protesters, Spider-Man-like, ascended the south tower and unfurled a gigantic FREE TIBET banner.

On Sunday, May 24, 1987, the pedestrianism got out of hand as far as crowd management was concerned. As part of the fiftieth anniversary celebration of its opening, the Bridge was closed to automobile traffic, and pedestrians were encouraged to walk across the Bridge from either the

San Francisco or Marin side in the early morning hours, to be followed later that morning by a parade of vintage cars: all this reminiscent of the two-day opening ceremonies of May 1937. As it was, some of the zaniness of the 1937 walk reccurred. A young woman in a Stanford sweatshirt, for example, planned to somersault her way across the Bridge. Four young men walked across on stilts. One young man in leopard-print underpants, a San Franciscan most obviously, stood in contrast to more modestly garbed Marinites; others wore signs around their necks indicating they had walked the Bridge as youngsters in 1937.

The pedestrian walk was scheduled to begin at 6:30 A.M., but by 5:30 A.M., the crowds on either side of the Bridge, swollen to unmanageability, spontaneously passed the restraining barriers and began their walk, sweeping along with them the San Francisco and Marin County officials who were supposed to preside at mid-Bridge ceremonies, which were never held. At mid-Bridge the San Francisco and Marin phalanxes met. Instead of passing each other on either side of the roadway as planned, the two phalanxes ran into each other head-on and came to a standstill, and the crowds behind them were brought to a halt in an increasingly impacted environment. By certain later estimates, the gridlocked crowd numbered some 250,000 pedestrians, which translated to a weight of roughly 4,800 pounds per lineal foot, for a total estimated weight of 31 million pounds of humanity on the basis of 125 pounds per person. Fortunately, a lighter roadway installed the previous year had increased the capacity of the Bridge to 5,800 pounds per lineal foot over its previous 4,000-pound capacity. Thus the Bridge held, although it flattened out and lost its characteristic arch. Winds of thirty to thirty-five miles per hour, meanwhile, were producing a decided sway in the roadbed, unnerving the crowd.

It is virtually beyond comprehension to contemplate what might have occurred—possibly the greatest man-made accident in human history—had the Bridge not been strengthened the previous year. As it was, the gridlocked crowd behaved with calm restraint as people waited, many of them for more than three hours, for harried officials to disperse the crowd from the rear and empty the Bridge north and south. So many human beings, pressed together in claustrophobic circumstances, many of them increasingly anxious regarding the swaying roadway, might have panicked and created a catastrophic crush, but this did not occur. On the contrary, aside from one or two alcohol-fueled fistfights on the margins of the crowd, not at the center, people behaved beautifully, and a disaster was avoided.

With the exception of one confirmed heart attack and one slightly serious bicycle accident during the dispersion phase, there was next to no report of serious health crises that could have proven disastrous, given the inability of medics to penetrate the crowd. A total of twenty-two children were reported separated from their parents, fifteen of them recovered or accounted for by mid-day: a source of terrible stress for parents, most obviously, but no children were reported hurt during their separation ordeal. Mid-morning the long-delayed parade of vintage cars began, led off by the same 1937 burgundy Cadillac convertible that had carried San Francisco mayor Angelo Rossi and California governor Frank Merriam across the Bridge fifty years earlier, now conveying San Francisco mayor Dianne Feinstein and her husband Richard Blum. There were fireworks that evening, and Tony Bennett and Carol Channing entertained at an outdoor concert on Crissy Field, also reprising the 1937 ceremonies.

Thus was the urban pedestrianism of the Golden Gate Bridge brought to unexpected extremes. No one—neither the District directors nor the staff of the Bridge, the Friends of the Golden Gate Bridge sponsoring the event, or for that matter the California Highway Patrol or the sheriffs of Marin and San Francisco counties—had come close to forecasting the size of the crowd that would show up for the commemorative ceremonies. In a sense, the size of the crowd came as an unwelcome surprise, as did the million-dollar debt incurred by the District for cleanup overtime and related expenses. Yet the overwhelming turnout, for all the problems it created, testified to the popularity of the Bridge as civic icon and pedestrian destination. Across one hectic, perilous, yet joyful morning, a million people celebrated their identification with a Bridge that conferred upon their metropolitan region its most compelling symbol of urban achievement, its City Beautiful, shared and triumphant.

-10-

SUICIDE

More troubling was the perennial and tragic problem of suicide. As the Bridge approached its fiftieth year, it had become second only to Mount Mihara, a volcano in Japan, as a place to commit suicide. By 2009 an estimated 1,300 people had thrown themselves from the Bridge to the waters below. Some put the figure as high as 1,400 or more, given the possibility of undetected nighttime jumps, with bodies swept by an outgoing tide to the waters off-shore, chum for sharks. By the first decade of the twenty-first century, then, an average of twenty-seven people a year were throwing themselves from the Bridge. A human body plunging 220 feet to the waters below reaches seventy-five to eighty miles per hour across a four-second fall and hits the water with an impact of fifteen thousand pounds per square inch, sufficient in most cases to puncture spleen, lungs, and heart with broken ribs; to sever the heart from the aorta; to snap vertebrae, rupture livers, and bring on a violent and instantaneous death; or, failing that, to plunge a maimed and unconscious jumper into the 350-foot-deep channel to drown; or, in even fewer instances, to be pulled broken and unconscious from the waters by the Coast Guard and die shortly thereafter.

The first person to end his life in this manner was a forty-nine-year-old bargeman by the name of H. B. Wobber, a veteran of the First World War. In August 1937, a few months after the Bridge opened, Wobber told another gentleman walking on the Bridge, "This is where I get off. I'm going to jump." Despite the fact that the other person in question, Professor Lewis Neylor from Trinity College, Connecticut, whom Wobber had met on the bus to the Bridge, grabbed his belt and tried to stop the proceedings, Wobber pulled away and threw himself over the barrier, achieving yet another Golden Gate Bridge first.

In earlier years, the press reported in some detail on each suicide, if at all possible, and from these cumulative reports emerged recurring variations of the genre: the divesting of coats, vests, or other outer clothing, in many cases folded neatly on the sidewalk, all of it constituting a preliminary ritual; or impulse suicides, with the suicide-to-be abruptly stopping his or her automobile mid-span, then darting over the rail. Cars parked at either the Marin or San Francisco entrance, preparatory to a walk and a jump at mid-span, were also part of the genre. In other cases, the suicide candidate would descend to a girder just beneath the fence and stand there before making the leap. Whatever the variation, most suicides occurred at mid-span or, if not there, closer in to the San Francisco side. Some suicides threw themselves backward from the railing or the girder below, but the majority tended to leap facing the city and the Bay. One gentleman was observed to hold his hat onto his head the entire way down.

A suicide note was frequently left behind in folded clothing or an automobile or secured with extra care in clothes worn into the water. As might be expected, reporters were especially interested in epigrammatic or otherwise well-written notes. "Survival of the fittest. Adios—unfit," scrawled on a Halloween card. This from a seventy-two-year-old pensioner, jumping off in 1954. "Why do they leave this so easy for suicide? Barbed wire would save a lot of lives." This from a well-to-do San Francisco apartment house owner in 1963. Many notes mentioned the Almighty, usually invoking His forgiveness and blessing on those left behind. Apologies were frequent, as were references to broken relationships, some of them poignant and wistful, others accusatory and bitter. ("You stacked the deck. Now you can enjoy a game of solitaire, because I am not playing.") References to health issues were frequent. ("I have cancer of the stomach. I am going nuts. I can't believe it. God forgive me.") Even a newly diagnosed case of arthritis could suffice. One note, from a forty-nine-year-old white male San Franciscan ("Absolutely no reason except I have a toothache") was retrieved from a coat left behind on the pavement and still holds honors as the most cryptic contribution to the genre.

The most painful were those notes in which the suicide condemned himself or herself, especially if he or she was young. Poignantly tragic was the young premed student from UCLA who followed his father off the Bridge just four days after his father's suicide in September 1954, leaving behind the note "I am sorry . . . I want to keep Dad company." In one case, that of a twenty-seven-year-old garbage collector in 1962, suicide followed the murder of a spouse. In one horrible instance—this from July 1945—a thirty-seven-year-old elevator installation foreman from San Francisco placed his five-year-old daughter on the girder, told her to jump, then followed her into the Bay, leaving behind the note "I and my daughter have committed suicide." In 1993 a man threw his three-year-old daughter off the Bridge, then jumped himself.

And so they went over the rail to their deaths: the noted

architect, the poet, the political fixer, the founder of Victoria's Secret; the respected and documented members of the middle class; the working men and women; those mourned by families and friends, some known to many, others seeming to come from nowhere, buried at public expense. No precise suicide profiles were kept in the early years, but in time—certainly by the early twenty-first century—a profile had emerged. Suicides from the Bridge tended to come from the Bay Area, indeed from the Bridge District itself, 85 percent of them. They were white, 80 percent of them, and male, 74.2 percent. Their average age was forty-one. Fully 56 percent of them had never married. The divorced and married were more or less equally balanced at 20 percent. A variety of occupations were listed, with student or teacher in the ascendancy, followed by homemaker, security guard, and, in later years, software engineer. Seventy-six percent had their exit demise witnessed, from the Bridge itself or from below.

In early decades, acceptance of the Bridge as an occasion for suicide was commonplace, appreciated with some humor, in point of fact, as part of the local color. *Chronicle* columnist Herb Caen, for example, noted on June 15, 1964, that while the Eiffel Tower had scored 330 suicides in seventy-five years, the Golden Gate Bridge had reached 262 in twenty-seven. Hooray for San Francisco! As that figure mounted, comparable statistics were written up in newspapers, and there were reports of betting pools. Some of this gallows humor, perhaps, represented an effort to ward off the sinister implications of the Golden Gate Bridge as a theater of death.

Defensively, some tried to suggest that San Francisco, indeed the entire Bay Area, was by definition a catchbasin, an alluvial plain, for the hopes and dreams of those arriving in search of a better life, hence an especially precarious place for those finding in the beauty and vitality of the region an intolerable judgment on their own unhappiness. Others charged that San Francisco itself was part of the problem, given its high rates of alcoholism and, in later times, its lack of sustaining family life among the population. In time, however, a more psychiatrically oriented explanation began to take hold. Like alcoholism itself, depression leading to suicide, it was argued, was a disease that might very well be genetically related.

While the orientation to suicide might be chronic or even inherited, the temptation to suicide, if resisted or thwarted, in a majority of cases led to a long-term containment of the urge to self-destruction. Statistically, the majority of suicide attempts by such means as poison or the slashing of wrists were failures. Hanging constituted a more certain technique. Suicide from the Golden Gate Bridge, by contrast, represented a virtually foolproof way to end it all. Four seconds and it was over. In the statistically negligible instances in which jumpers survived, however, they reported that the millisecond they were off the Bridge, they regretted their decision. Hundreds of others must have had the same regret, to no avail.

Far from being an inevitability, a tendency to self-destruct was increasingly being seen as a treatable disease. From the 1950s onward, gaining strength with the century, the psychiatric interpretation of suicide as preventable motivated among anti-suicide activists and other mental health groups a campaign against the perception of suicides from the Golden Gate Bridge as a form of public theater, morbidly operatic, in which the Bridge offered a bizarrely romanticized means of self-destruction. The detailed reporting of these suicides in the press, activists argued, reinforced a macabre sense of accepted social ritual. The attention paid to Golden Gate Bridge suicides, in newspaper stories especially, had created a self-perpetuating genre attached to place, the Golden Gate Bridge, in which emotionally or mentally afflicted individuals perceived the Bridge—as others perceived the Eiffel Tower or the Empire State Building—not only as the means for ending life, but as a speciously romanticized place to carry it out with a certain amount of high drama. As the most famous bridge in the world, a triumph of site, art, engineering, and social statement, the Bridge by its very definition lent itself to such an identity, however morbid, enhanced by widespread press coverage. By the late twentieth century, suicide-prevention activists and the Bridge board of directors as well, in an effort to counter the identity of the Bridge as Suicide Central, had successfully discouraged detailed press reports of Bridge suicides—with the exception of well-known personalities—and discussions of cumulative numbers and comparative statistics with other favored suicide places. By the 1990s suicide from the Golden Gate Bridge had ceased as a localized spectator sport.

Still, the suicides continued, driving the 262 figure of June 1964 to the 1,300 or more figure of 2009. Starting in the 1950s, the ease of committing suicide off the Bridge—an easy climb over a four-foot-high fence—motivated a half-century debate over the installation of some form of suicide barrier. In the early twentieth century, pro-barrier activists pointed out, the Colorado Bridge across the Arroyo Seco in Pasadena had likewise been a bridge of choice for suicides in the Los Angeles region. The installation of a suicide barrier, however, had reduced suicides from the Colorado Bridge to nil. Anti-suicide barriers on the Eiffel Tower and Empire State Building showed similar results. Why not do the same for the Golden Gate? Suggestions included increasing the height of the four-foot railings, so easy for suicides to sur-mount (designed that way, some alleged, because Joseph Strauss was barely more than five feet tall), either by replac-ing them with a new barrier or running a second fence across the top. Second in importance, as far as support was concerned, was the construction of a steel mesh net projected twenty feet outward beneath the roadways from supportive girders. Such a net would not violate the aesthetics of the Bridge, it was argued, the way that increasing the roadway fence would, thereby countering a repeated objection to a surface barrier on the grounds that it would destroy the aesthetics of the Bridge.

Back and forth the debate continued, decade by decade, through a number of studies reluctantly undertaken by the directors. Finally, after seventy years of tireless advocacy by anti-suicide and mental health activists such as the Bridge Rail Foundation and the Marin Suicide Prevention Center—augmented by testimony from a young man, bipolar, who had jumped, regretted it instantly, and survived to tell the tale—the directors in the summer of 2009 approved the construction of a steel-cable net twenty feet below the Bridge span. The problem was: the directors also mandated that no Bridge fund revenues could be used on the $50 million project. This restriction sent safety-net supporters scrambling for federal funds that, as of August 2009, would not be available for an additional eighteen months, if they were ever to be available at all.

In the meantime, suicides from the Bridge most likely would continue, ignored in most cases by the press, true, yet still possessed of a certain morbid fascination, as Eric

Steel's 2006 film *The Bridge* painfully documented. Inspired by an article by Tad Friend in the October 13, 2003, *New Yorker*, "Jumpers: The Fatal Grandeur of the Golden Gate Bridge," Steel and his crew spent much of 2004 maintaining surveillance of the Bridge, filming suspicious figures—those leaning overlong against the barrier, or pacing restlessly back and forth—on digital video. When some critics later attacked *The Bridge* as a form of morbid voyeurism, Steel countered that his crew had helped to prevent six suicides by reporting them to Bridge security. At least one thwarted suicide was filmed, a young woman pulled back from the girder by a young and fit white male passerby. But at least two successful leaps were documented on camera, one by a tall late-middle-aged white man in a tracksuit who climbed abruptly over the barrier. The second—a white rocker type in his mid-thirties, dressed in black, with long hair, blown by the wind, which he was continually brushing from his face—was a more obvious candidate for self-destruction, returning as he did again and again to the rail from his pacing on the roadway, staring gloomily into the Bay, the city, the Berkeley hills in the distance, before launching himself into an eerily graceful backward dive.

The bulk of Steel's film, it must be noted, consisted of the grief-ridden commentary of survivors: parents, siblings, friends, each a secondary victim to one degree or another. *The Bridge* can hence legitimately be defended as an anti-suicide tract despite criticisms to the contrary. No film, however, has more lyrically evoked the beauty of the Bridge, permanent in steel, triumphant in color, evanescent in billowing fog across cycles of time and weather. Brilliantly filmed and edited, hauntingly scored, replete with life-affirming imagery of people enjoying their stroll across the span, *The Bridge* paradoxically reinforces the very enigma it seeks to dispel: beauty and life linked to death, engineering and architecture soaring over a void into which troubled people launch themselves.

-11-

ART

The shimmering, seductive beauty of Eric Steel's *The Bridge* underscores the tragedy of suicide. At the same time, it reveals the Bridge as *la belle dame sans merci*, a beautiful lady without mercy. Beauty at once calls to life—and to death, for those so inclined. The complexity and ambiguity of Steel's film help structure it into the most successful, if troubling, artistic interpretation of the Golden Gate Bridge to date. To say this is not to claim too much. In contrast to the Brooklyn Bridge, the Golden Gate Bridge has not inspired an impressive amount of art or interpretive response. The Bridge itself, first of all, is its own best statement. Striking, enigmatic, the Bridge represents the best possible symbol of its achievement. Thus it participates in the autonomy and transcendence of art. So complete is the Bridge unto itself, no genre of art or criticism—at least up until now—has shown itself able to interpret it better than it interprets itself.

Photography, and by extension filmmaking, remain qualified exceptions to this judgment, for they most directly allow the Bridge to speak for itself. Linked to the visual, painting possesses a similar advantage. The Golden Gate Bridge, however, has not yet inspired any paintings remotely comparable to Joseph Stella's freestanding *Brooklyn Bridge* (ca. 1919) or *The Bridge*, the last panel of Stella's heroic five-panel *The Voice of the City of New York Interpreted* (1920–22). Nor has the Golden Gate Bridge inspired any poem in the league of Hart Crane's *The Bridge* (1930). This is not to say that comparable poems or paintings will not one day be achieved, should the requisite artists be on hand and should the Golden Gate Bridge inspire them, as the Brooklyn Bridge inspired Stella and Crane. Until that day arrives, however, the record of interpretive and artistic responses to the Golden Gate Bridge must be judged for what it is: a promise of better things to come.

Efforts at interpretation began as early as 1846 with Frémont's naming of the site Chrysopylae, Golden Gate, in reference to the Golden Horn of Constantinople, a designation fraught with a metaphor destined to unfold over time. Here would be a city, Frémont suggested, in which artists, philosophers, and poets would one day flourish. In 1879, thirty-three years after Frémont named the site but long before the Bridge was even thought of, the Golden Gate inspired a hopeful young philosopher by the name of Josiah Royce, then teaching at Berkeley, to resolve to dedicate his life to the big questions. "With these problems," vowed Royce, regarding the great issues of mind and nature, as he sat atop a Berkeley hilltop, gazing across the Bay to the Golden Gate, "I shall seek to busy myself earnestly, because that is each one's duty; independently, because I am a Californian, as little bound to follow mere tradition as I am liable to find an audience by preaching in this wilderness; reverently, because I am thinking and writing face to face with a mighty and lovely Nature, by the side of whose greatness I am but a worm." Thus the Golden Gate provided the aspiring young philosopher, destined to emerge in his maturity as a giant in his field, with both the setting and the symbol for his life's work.

A half century later, during the very process of envisioning the Bridge, artists played a role. San Francisco painter Maynard Dixon first suggested what the Bridge might look like, even as it was in the process of being designed. San Francisco sculptor Beniamino Bufano led the campaign to choose International Orange as its permanent color. Scenic designer John Eberson and architect Irving Morrow fused

their talents with those of engineers Leon Moisseiff and
Charles Alton Ellis to create the Bridge as work of art. In
1934 the noted landscapist Ray Strong, a student of Dixon's
living in San Francisco at the time, painted the Bridge under
construction: a south-to-north view, the Marin tower rising in the distance against green-brown hills from Bay
waters of blue and green, and in the foreground the massive
concrete anchorages, recently stripped of their scaffolding,
framing the red brick walls of Fort Point. The Bridge completed, the noted woodcut artists Mallette Dean and Otis
Oldfield captured the geometric power of the Bridge structure, up close at angles or from a near distance, steady and
serene as in a Japanese painting, inseparable from the site
itself.

Commissioned by the federal government, Strong's painting was chosen by President Roosevelt to hang in the White
House and remained there for many years before being
transferred in 1965 by the Park Service of the Department
of the Interior to the Smithsonian American Art Museum,
testimony to its artistic and documentary force. In achieving this, Strong was anticipating the photographers—the
father-and-sons team of Gabriel, Irving, and Raymond
Moulin; the independent photographer Peter Stackpole;
Ted Huggins, working for Standard Oil; and George
Dixon of Tidewater Associated Oil—who documented
the construction of the Bridge, mounting its rising heights

to photograph work and workers, cable and steel, or in Dixon's case shooting from the open rear seat of a biplane to capture the emerging, massive totality of the structure. The 1930s was a golden age of documentarian photography; and while lesser known today than many of their counterparts, these Bridge photographers won a place for themselves in the history of photography with their cumulative documentation of Bridge construction in sharply focused black and white. The term *cumulative* is appropriate because no single photographer caught it all. Their total effort, rather, chronicles the epic: Ansel Adams's last lingering look through the Gate in its primal condition, the tractors and steam shovels moving earth at Fort Point and the Marin Headlands; the beehive geometry of crisscrossed steel rods awaiting the pouring of concrete; the emergence of massive eyebars from concrete anchorages; the struggle against the sea to establish the south tower; the rising of the towers themselves in a progression of geometric cells; the spinning of cables; the dropping of suspender lines; the final definition being achieved by the roadway as it advances east and west in two sections toward the center; and the men, the construction workers, weather-beaten and grizzled beyond their chronological age after lifetimes of hard work in the outdoors, their concrete- and paint-spattered boots and overalls, their military-style leather helmets, their smiling faces revealing uneven, silver-capped teeth.

Views also were provided of the rising Bridge from different vantage points: in the distance glimpsed through a screen of eucalyptus leaves; observed from the air, narrow and soaring across the strait; encountered at water level, a passenger ship or freighter passing serenely beneath the unfinished structure. The photographers caught it all in the full confidence that their medium was totally congruent with the occasion, fully able to allow the girders, cable, concrete, and soaring towers to speak for themselves as they flowed into a total composition, and the grizzled and sinewy men to be themselves as they tended to their work. Epic force, epic grandeur even, pervades the best of these photographs, with their ability, as in the case of all epics, to let men, nature, and things speak directly for themselves.

Self-conscious aesthetics, by contrast, even a concern for the picturesque, are almost totally absent from the photographic record of the 1930s. These values would arrive in a later era as a second and third generation of photographers engaged the completed Bridge. The Golden Gate Bridge pages at the Web site art.com tell the story across hundreds of images from the post-war period currently available for sale through this cyber-gallery. Poster art promoting travel falls out of use during World War II for obvious reasons, but by the 1950s the Bridge is reappearing in travel posters, most notably those of the Matson Line, operating the *Mariposa* and *Monterey* between Honolulu and San Francisco, and

TWA, linking the Bay Area to the rest of the country and the Asia/Pacific Basin. The use of the Bridge for advertising and promotion begins to gain momentum. A line of ballerinas in full attire dances beneath the Bridge at Fort Point to promote the San Francisco Ballet, this from the early 1950s. A 1957 LP from Fantasy Studios in Berkeley features pianist Vince Guaraldi in full view of the south tower and has much to do with making *Jazz Impressions* not only a bestseller but a quintessential LP when it came to evoking the Bay Area jazz scene in this era. By the twenty-first century, the Bridge had become a staple of magazine and television advertising, for automobiles most notably, as appropriate, but also for a Tempur-Pedic mattress on which a young lady is blissfully sleeping on a bed on a hill overlooking the Marin approach.

Non-commercial photography resumed its course in the 1940s in a somewhat retro documentarian style, taking up the approach in use before Pearl Harbor. In the 1950s, with abstract expressionism in vogue, photographers began to search for unusual angles and compositions and tended to emphasize the engineering structure of the Bridge in conjunction with its natural setting. Concurrent with these developments, the second generation of Bridge photographers, working in the post-war era through the 1960s, increasingly saw the Bridge in terms of its relationship to San Francisco: this at a time when tourism was becoming, and was by 1962, the lead element in the San Francisco economy. This conjunction of Bridge and city continued with an emphasis on Bay recreation—yachts with sails billowing, windsurfers, a yoga class on the beach—all this with the Bridge in view. In the 1980s the picturesque came increasingly into ascendancy. Fog and the Bridge, sunrise, and sunset were favored occasions, as evident in sumptuous books of San Francisco photography published by Abrams and Rizzoli.

Photography, then, emerged as the dominant art form with which to celebrate the Bridge. The transition to film documentary was inevitable. Over the years, the Bridge has received frequent documentary treatment, whether as part of the larger Bay Area scene—as in the case of the award-winning *Above San Francisco* (1973), narrated by Orson Welles—or in Ben Loeterman's *Golden Gate Bridge* (2004), part of the *American Experience* series on PBS television. Combining historical footage of construction, interviews with surviving Bridge builders and various experts, and a vivid presentation of the Bridge in contemporary life, Loeterman's PBS film remains the single best documentary of its kind: informed, historically accurate, elegantly photographed.

As might be expected, Hollywood made effective use of the Bridge as mise-en-scène. The Bridge is the goal of the malfunctioning passenger plane from Hawaii piloted by

John Wayne in *The High and the Mighty* (1954). A giant octopus makes havoc of the south tower in *It Came from Beneath the Sea* (1955). Kim Novak throws herself into the Bay at the south end of the Bridge and is rescued by Jimmy Stewart in *Vertigo* (1958). In the aftermath of World War III, submarine captain Gregory Peck surveys the Bridge through a periscope in *On the Beach* (1959) as the eerily empty entry to a Bay Area whose population has succumbed to radiation sickness. The Bridge provides background for *Flower Drum Song* (1961) and *Guess Who's Coming to Dinner* (1967). Carroll O'Connor meets his end in Fort Point in *Point Blank* (1967). George C. Scott and Julie Christie walk beneath the Bridge at Fort Point in *Petulia* (1968). Helen Hayes is given a terrifying ride up and down one of the cables in *Herbie Rides Again* (1974), the sequel to *The Love Bug*. The San Andreas Fault collapses and Christopher Reeve saves a school bus full of children from falling off the Bridge into the Bay in *Superman* (1978). In the 1980s Hollywood seems to have taken a break from the Bridge but returned in full force in the 1990s to use it as a setting in such films as *Tales of the City* (1993), *Mrs. Doubtfire* (1993), *Dream for an Insomniac* (1996), *Nine Months* (1995), *Sweet November* (2001), and *Doctor Doolittle 2* (2001). In most of these films over the decades, the Bridge and views of the Bridge are employed as picturesque settings and delineations of place in films that do not possess a plot strongly dependent upon San Francisco. *Vertigo*, however, represents an exception, with Alfred Hitchcock using San Francisco not only as a setting but also as the partial theme of his enigmatic story.

The Golden Gate Bridge is not destroyed in *On the Beach*, only eerily empty in a Bay Area devastated by atomic fallout. Yet the destruction of the Bridge by malevolent action has remained a reccurring fear since the immediate aftermath of Pearl Harbor, when it was widely expected throughout the Bay Area that the Japanese would next be attacking the coast. In the novel *The Golden Gate* (1976) British thrillmeister Alistair MacLean—author of the best-selling *The Guns of Navarone* (1957), equally successful as a motion picture—brings such fears to full consciousness in a detailed depiction of the seizure of the Bridge by a band of international criminals demanding ransom money from the federal government with a threat to blow the towers to oblivion. Overly contrived as a thriller—with a plot involving the kidnapping of the president of the United States and various cabinet members, along with the king of Saudi Arabia, touring the Bridge in the course of a state visit—MacLean's novel never made the screen and remains among his more forgettable efforts. The novel did, however, vividly suggest the vulnerability of the Bridge to terrorist attack long before the events of 9/11 sent reinforcing cadres of National Guard and Highway Patrol to the Bridge in fear that it was targeted along with the World Trade

Center for destruction. Since 9/11, the security of the Golden Gate Bridge has remained the highest priority with District, state, and federal agencies, fully aware of the attractiveness of the iconic Golden Gate Bridge as a target of terrorist attack; indeed, as in the case of so many other American icons, anxiety over such an attack—its probability, some claim—remains attached to the Bridge.

For all practical purposes, the Golden Gate Bridge functions in a manner similar to the Statue of Liberty, announcing in its case American civilization to the Asia/Pacific Basin as well as embodying the westward march of that civilization across the continent in the nineteenth century. Because that westward march was so horrendously flawed in its treatment of Native Americans, the Bridge cannot function as an unequivocal icon of American destiny; indeed, Native American activists came as close to seizing the Bridge as they could when in November 1969 they seized the island of Alcatraz, deactivated six years prior as the site of a maximum security federal prison. The Native Americans eventually left, however, and Alcatraz prison became one of the most popular destinations in the national park system. This popularity shelved all plans to tear down the prison and erect on Alcatraz an Asia/Pacific-oriented Statue of Liberty, welcoming one and all into San Francisco Bay.

In October 1936 Cardinal Eugenio Pacelli, Vatican secretary of state, soon to assume office as Pope Pius XII, blessed the Bridge, nearing completion, in the course of a visit to the West Coast. The blessing pleased Catholics in what was then a very Catholic town. No formal blessing was required, however, for the Bridge to develop in its own way as a symbol of deeper realities. Most dramatically, the Bridge served as an agonizing or exhilarating psychological symbol for the more than 1.2 million servicemen and -women who sailed beneath it during World War II and for those who did likewise during the Korean War or for those soldiers and Marines who saw it from the air as their chartered World Airways or Flying Tiger plane took off from the Oakland Airport, banked westward across both bridges, and headed to Vietnam. Seen upon departure, whether from the channel or the air, the Golden Gate Bridge expressed the life left behind and the fearsome dangers to come. Seen upon return, the Bridge suggested safe harbor, recovery, the joy of life in years that now would be theirs.

In a most unusual novel, *The Golden Gate* (1986), narrated entirely through linked sonnets, the Indian novelist and poet Vikram Seth depicts that continuing search for the good life, Bay Area style, in a narrative linking the lives of young San Franciscans. A longtime graduate student in economics at Stanford, where he was also a Wallace Stegner Fellow in Creative Writing, Seth knew from firsthand experience the class background of his urban professional protagonists and the city in which they were pursuing love and career. While the Golden Gate Bridge itself is the exclusive subject of only one sonnet, it functions as a signature symbol, a branding, for the entire region, from Palo Alto to Napa, centered on San Francisco, in which privileged members of the boomer generation fall in and out of love, organize start-ups, deal with aging parents, plan and attend art gallery openings, and otherwise suggest San Francisco as a mega-city for ambitious professionals living in an environment at once competitive and conducive to the joy of life.

There is little of the heroic in the lives and loves of Seth's protagonists, only the challenges of every day. From this perspective, the Golden Gate of his title, at once the Bridge and the region, evokes the Bridge, for all its engineering and architectural grandeur, as an accepted and familiar backdrop for daily life. This same sense of the Bridge as a recognized part of Bay Area life pervades the effort of the Bay Area songwriting team of Bob Voss and Noah Griffin, whose song "The Bridge: Golden Gate" (2007) suggests the Bridge as an easy, available source of continuity and comfort for Bay Area residents in one or another stage of life's journey. Even San Francisco architect Donald MacDonald, the direct heir of Irving Morrow—responsible for, among other projects, the redesign of the Bridge's light fixtures, the relighting of the towers, the bike rail, and various suicide-prevention proposals—manages in his authoritative *Golden Gate Bridge: History and Design of an Icon* (2008) to render the Bridge as an accessible aspect of the Bay Area landscape and environment, serving everyday purposes, as well as an instance of high engineering and architecture. In *The Golden Gate Bridge Troll* (1978), meanwhile, children's author Jean Fitzgerald has even further domesticated the Bridge with a charming story of a benevolent troll who keeps the Bridge in working order.

All this contrasts with the heroic rhetoric, whether in prose or poetry, surrounding the Bridge in its early years, beginning with Bridge director Francis Keesling's dedication address and Joseph Strauss's dedicatory poem, "The Mighty Task Is Done." A digest of themes, in fact, can easily be assembled from these early efforts: the nobility of the site, the appropriateness of the Bridge to the environment, the Bridge as social and cultural symbol, the heroism of Bridge construction workers. Robin Lampson's "The Mending of a Continent" (1937) celebrates the dual dedication of the San Francisco–Oakland Bay and Golden Gate bridges with a depiction of the bridges as living entities.

> *These delicate-powerful towers and cables and spans*
>   *are the living*
> *Warm skeleton of our race's embodied aspiration*
>   *and intelligence and achievement:*

These muscular structures shall breathe the traffic
of nations, feel the tides
Of mankind as a lifeblood, be clothed
in our consciousness of humanity's power.

Stanton Coblentz's "From the Golden Gate Bridge" (1947) introduces a welcome note of humility in its acknowledgment that, despite the power of the Bridge, nature retained its primacy, as time would inevitably tell.

This shall remain: the ragged headlands flung
Far out against the sunset-crimsoned sea;
Dim spits and isles; and one star-lantern hung
Over the wrinkled, long immensity;
These clouds that flare from ruby-red to gray;
Those peaks that stab the violet dusk; and white
Of breakers curving in wide lips of spray
Under the bald and seagull-peopled height.

For all its apparent permanence—for all of Joseph Strauss's promises to A. P. Giannini that it would last forever—the Golden Gate Bridge is anchored in time and as such is time-determined, hence vulnerable and subject to decay. The Bridge defies time but is destined to lose its battle, even if hundreds of years into the future, as so many of the Seven Wonders of the Ancient World have lost theirs; just as, in point of fact, the mountain ridge that once sealed off the Golden Gate lost its battle with water-driven erosion in the distant geological past. Wind, fog, the pressures of tidal action, the natural erosions of weather, the pounding impact of ceaseless automotive traffic, the vulnerability of steel to its maritime environment: all this necessitates constant maintenance and repair. Left unattended or haphazardly maintained, left unreinforced in its roadbed or unreplaced in its suspender cables, or seismically unreinforced in its towers, the Bridge would have long since been showing signs of the ruin it would eventually become.

In this regard, a major earthquake poses the most dangerous threat to the Bridge, placed as it is so adjacent to the San Andreas Fault. On October 17, 1989, the 7.1 magnitude Loma Prieta earthquake provided the District with a compelling challenge verging on a wake-up call. With its epicenter located some sixty miles to the south, the Loma Prieta quake caused no discernible damage to the Golden Gate Bridge. It fractured, however, a portion of the upper deck of the San Francisco–Oakland Bay Bridge, causing several cars to fall to the lower deck (with one fatality), and this constituted a grave warning to the District. The sheer havoc wrought by Loma Prieta—sixty-eight deaths, at least 3,700 injuries, between $6 billion and $7 billion in property damage and related costs—focused the attention of the Golden Gate Bridge community of directors, consultants, public officials, and commuters on the seismic safety of the fifty-two-year-old landmark structure. Should an earthquake comparable to Loma Prieta strike closer to the site, how would the Bridge fare? Not so well, replied the U.S. Geological Survey and other scientific organizations. Even before Loma Prieta the USGS had pointed out that there was a 62 percent probability that an earthquake of 6.7 magnitude or greater would strike the Bay Area within the next thirty years. The effect of such a quake on the Bridge should be immediately and extensively studied.

Loma Prieta fast-forwarded the process. Among other consultants, the District retained the globally ranked civil engineering firm of T. Y. Lin International, based in San Francisco, to prepare a seismic evaluation of the Bridge. Filed in July 1991, the Lin report, together with other related studies, was sobering. A 7.0 magnitude earthquake near the Bridge would damage and close it for an extended period of time. An 8.0 or greater quake might very well bring down the two approach viaducts and the Fort Point arch and do catastrophic damage to the suspension structure. Since the cost (an estimated $1.4 billion) and the long-term disruption of replacing the Bridge rendered such an option out of the question, the District embarked upon studies resulting in a three-phase, multi-million-dollar seismic retrofit scheduled for completion in 2013. Phase One, completed in December 2001 at a cost of $71 million, paid for by the toll fees, involved the virtual reconstruction of the Marin approach viaduct. Completed in the spring of 2008 at the cost of $189 million in federal, state, and regional funds, Phase Two retrofitted the multiple structures comprising the San Francisco approach, including the Fort Point arch. Launched in April 2008, Phase Three involved the expenditure of some $400 million in federal funds and regional and state earmarks in an ambitious effort to retrofit the north anchorage and pylon, the main towers and suspension span, and the south tower pier and fender over five or more years of modification and reconstruction. In each phase, Donald MacDonald Architects insured that all engineering conform to the design standards of the 1937 structure.

Constant maintenance, meanwhile, continued its role in the counterattack against time and dissolution. Over the decades, the Bridge has been continually painted and repainted by a permanent painting crew so as to preserve its coat of International Orange, which in turn protects its steel. A daily and equally continuous inspection locates loose or frayed bolts or hairline fissures in one or another steel fastening, however small and insignificant. Over time, the roadway has been continually repaved. In 1986 it was replaced entirely with a lighter, stronger structure. Workers, meanwhile, walk the cables, ever alert to any irregularity, fine-tune the elevator, arrange and rearrange lane dividers according to the ebb and flow of traffic. From the perspective of its maintenance, the Bridge is at once a grand and permanent thing, destined for the ages, and an airliner in flight, dependent upon repeated cycles of maintenance and replacement.

In struggling on behalf of the durability of the Golden Gate Bridge, maintenance workers can take satisfaction in the fact that the Great Pyramid of Egypt still rises from the desert floor and water still comes into the gardens of Rome through an aqueduct built in classical times. But the Colossus that once loomed over the entrance to the harbor at Rhodes now lies in fragments at the bottom of the Aegean, and the mausoleum at Halicarnassus is today a heap of stones in the Turkish city of Bodrum. Still, comfort is afforded by those wonders that have survived, as well as by the Great Wall of China, Hadrian's Wall, the great stupas of Sri Lanka, Java, and Burma, the Pantheon in Rome, the Hagia Sophia in Istanbul, and the other iconic structures of the planet that have survived because they are durable and in many cases properly used and cherished. Given its seismic retrofit and maintenance program, there is every reason to believe that the Golden Gate Bridge will last for centuries to come, barring natural or man-made disasters.

Yet science predicts that a great earthquake will one day strike, against which the District has embarked upon its ambitious program of seismic defense. The entire Bay Area, however, lives under this same threat and goes about its ordinary business in a condition of acceptance verging upon denial, allowing the future, for the time being, to remain exactly that: an inevitability, true, but capable of being defended against by innovative engineering. And as far as terrorism is concerned, that possibility now also lurks in the borderlands of our conscious and subconscious awareness, an ominously imagined Trojan Horse that despite our best efforts may one day gain entrance to the city.

Still, for the time being—and that time being could last for centuries—the Golden Gate Bridge remains a world icon. What does the Bridge mean, finally, after each of its engineering and architectural achievements is explored? As in the case of all great art, there remains an element of mystery. Like a Bach fugue, or Beethoven's Ninth, or a symphony by Mahler, the Golden Gate Bridge can be analyzed in terms of its parts and functions. In its final effect and meaning, however, the Bridge is more than the sum total of any of these. The Golden Gate Bridge embodies a beauty at once useful and transcendent. It emanates a music of mathematics and design and offers enduring proof that human beings can alter the planet with reverence, can mend or complete their environment for social purposes. The Bridge is a triumphant structure, a testimony to the creativity of mankind. At the same time, it also asserts the limits and brevity of human achievement in a cosmos that is as endless and ancient as time itself.

ESSAY ON SOURCES

1: Bridge

Regarding the great bridges of the world, see H. Shirley Smith, *The World's Great Bridges* (revised edition, 1964); and Judith Dupré, *Bridges: A History of the World's Most Famous and Important Spans* (1997). See also Henry Petroski, *Engineers of Dreams: Great Bridge Builders and the Spanning of America* (1995). Regarding the impact of the Brooklyn Bridge on the American imagination, see Wanda M. Corn, *The Great American Thing: Modern Art and National Identity, 1915–1935* (1999). For the text and background to Hart Crane's *The Bridge* (1930), see *Hart Crane: Complete Poems and Selected*

Letters, edited by Langdon Hammer (Library of America, 2006). Two valuable explications of Crane's complex poem are Waldo Frank, *The Bridge: A Poem by Hart Crane* (1933); and Alan Trachtenberg, "Cultural Revisions in the Twenties: Brooklyn Bridge as 'Usable Past,'" in *The American Self: Myth, Ideology, and Popular Culture*, edited by Sam B. Girgus (1981), 58–75.

2: Icon

The most comprehensive histories of the Golden Gate Bridge are Richard Thomas Loomis, "The History of the Building of the Golden Gate Bridge," PhD dissertation, Department of History, Stanford University, 1958 (University Microfilms, 1959); Allen Brown, *Golden Gate: Biography of a Bridge* (1965); John Van der Zee, *The Gate: The True Story of the Design and Construction of the Golden Gate Bridge* (1986); Charles F. Adams, *Heroes of the Golden Gate* (1987); and Louise Nelson Dyble, *Paying the Toll: Local Power, Regional Politics, and the Golden Gate Bridge* (2009). See also James W. Schock, *The Bridge: A Celebration. The Golden Gate Bridge at Sixty, 1937–1997* (1997). Regarding Joseph Strauss, see Michael Chester, *Joseph Strauss: Builder of the Golden Gate Bridge* (1965). Also of great use is Golden Gate Bridge Highway and Transportation District, *Highlights, Facts & Figures* (fifth edition, July 2000).

3: Site

Of central importance to any comprehensive understanding of the site is the essay "A Hidden Geography" by Richard Walker included in the photographic album *Richard Misrach: Golden Gate* (second edition, 2005), 145–58. For further background to the Golden Gate, see Neill C. Wilson, *Here Is the Golden Gate* (1962). Regarding the northward advance of Spain into the Bay Area, see David J. Weber, *The Spanish Frontier in North America* (1992). See also the first volume of the seven-volume *History of California* by Henry Lebbeus Oak, volume 18 of *The Works of Hubert Howe Bancroft* (39 volumes, 1883–90). See also Zoeth Skinner Eldredge, *The Beginnings of San Francisco* (2 volumes, 1912). Also of value is the WPA/Hastings House guide *San Francisco: The Bay and Its Cities*, new revised edition, edited by Gladys Hansen (1973), part of the American Guide Series.

4: Vision

The Bridge was initially announced by Joseph Strauss and Michael O'Shaughnessy in the brochure *Bridging "the Golden Gate"* (1921). Strauss himself fully elaborated his vision of the Bridge in his September 1937 *The Golden Gate Bridge: Report of the Chief Engineer to the Board of Directors of the Golden Gate Bridge and Highway District* (50th Anniversary Edition, 1987). See also the pre-construction pamphlet *The Golden Gate*

Bridge: Synopsis of the Report of the Chief Engineer (ca. 1930). Regarding Frank Doyle, see Ira B. Cross, *Financing an Empire: History of Banking in California* (four volumes, 1927), 4:395–97.

5: Politics

Regarding the early political history of the Bridge, Loomis's PhD dissertation, Van der Zee's *The Gate*, and Dyble's *Paying the Toll* have proven especially useful. Opposition by the Pacific American Steamship Association is evident in its published brief *Protest of Pacific American Steamship Association and Shipowners' Association of the Pacific Coast Before the Board of Officers Appointed by Chief of Engineers of the United States Army in the Matter of the Application of Golden Gate Bridge and Highway District for Approval of Plans for Construction of a Bridge Across the Golden Gate* (1930).

6: Money

Richard Loomis provides the most complete chronicle of the financing of the Bridge.

7: Design

The full design and program for the Bridge was released as Golden Gate Bridge and Highway District, *The Golden Gate Bridge at San Francisco, California: Report of the Chief Engineer, with Architectural Studies, to the Board of Directors, Golden Gate*

Bridge and Highway District (three volumes, August 27, 1930). When it comes to design issues, Donald MacDonald and Ira Nadel's *Golden Gate Bridge: History and Design of an Icon*, illustrations by Donald MacDonald (2008), commands the field. For a contemporary introduction, see Golden Gate Bridge and Highway District, *The Golden Gate Bridge: History and Principal Characteristics* (1933).

8: Construction

Regarding the steel structure of the Bridge, the illustrated brochure *The Golden Gate Bridge* issued by the Bethlehem Steel Company (1937) is most useful. See also the promotional brochure *Treasure Island and the World's Greatest Spans of Steel* (1939). In addition to Loomis, Van der Zee, and Dyble, the following are especially valuable regarding the construction of the Bridge: *High Steel: Building the Bridges Across San Francisco Bay,* text by Richard Dillon, photographs edited by Don DeNevi and Thomas Moulin (1979); *Baron Wolman Presents Spanning the Gate*, text by Stephen Cassady (1979); and *Superspan*, photography by Baron Wolman, text by Tom Horton (1983). For a construction worker's perspective, see John V. Robinson, *Al Zampa and the Bay Area Bridges* (Images of America, 2005). See also the valuable contemporary pamphlet by E. Cromwell Mensch, *The Golden Gate Bridge: A Technical Description in Ordinary Language* (1935). Regarding the construction of the San Francisco–Oakland Bay Bridge, see

Paul Trimble and John C. Alioto Jr., *The Bay Bridge* (Images of America, 2004). Regarding the strengthening of the Bridge roadway in 1953, see Clifford Paine, Othmar Ammann, and Charles Andrew, *Report on Alterations of Golden Gate Bridge by Board of Engineers* (1953).

9: City

Donald MacDonald briefly links the Bridge to the City Beautiful movement. See also "The City Beautiful and the San Francisco Fair," in Kevin Starr's *Americans and the California Dream, 1850–1915* (1973). Regarding the Philopolis movement, see Harvey L. Jones, *The Art of Arthur and Lucia Mathews*, foreword by Kevin Starr (2006). Regarding the fiesta celebrating the dedication of the Bridge, see the *Gold Book: Golden Gate Bridge Fiesta Official Guide and Directory* (1937). See also Golden Gate Bridge and Highway District, *First Annual Report of Operations* (June 1938). Regarding the recreational development of the site, see Amy Meyer with Randolph Delehanty, *New Guardians for the Golden Gate: How America Got a Great National Park*, foreword by I. Michael Heyman (2006). For the fiftieth anniversary pedestrian debacle, see the special editions of the *San Francisco Chronicle* and the *Marin Independent Journal* for May 25, 1987, for extensive coverage. For a comprehensive survey of the Bridge in its fiftieth year of operation, see the *Marin Independent*

Journal special publication *A View of the Bridge: 50 Years Spanning the Golden Gate* (1987).

For an overall history of the transportation programs of the District, see "Transit History: Birth of the Golden Gate Bus and Ferry Transit System," http://www.goldengate transit.org/researchlibrary/history.php. Two crucial Golden Gate Bridge District reports are Philip F. Spaulding and Associates, *Golden Gate Commuter Ferryboat System, San Francisco–Marin Crossing* (August 1970) and *Five Year Transit Development Plan* (June 1980). Regarding Doyle Drive improvements, see San Francisco County Transportation Authority, *Doyle Drive: South Access to the Golden Gate Bridge: Citizens' Guide to the Draft Environmental Impact Statement/Report* (December 2005). Regarding the Doyle Drive plan chosen by the District, see Michael Cabanatuan, "Three Years of Detours for Doyle Drive Fix," *San Francisco Chronicle* and SFGate.com, July 25, 2009.

10: Suicide

Regarding the history of suicide from the Bridge, see Allen Brown, *Golden Gate*, 192–223. See also the Bridge Rail Foundation, *A Ten-Year Report: Golden Gate Bridge Suicide Demographics* (2007). The *New Yorker* published Tad Friend's "Jumpers: The Fatal Grandeur of the Golden Gate Bridge" on October 13, 2003. Regarding Eric Steel's film *The Bridge*, see Stephen Holden's review "That Beautiful but Deadly San Francisco Span" in the *New York Times* for October 27, 2006, and Jim Emerson's review of the same date at rogerebert. com. See also the Bridge Rail Foundation report for September 2009 at bridgerail.org. Regarding the authorization of a safety net, see Will Reisman, "Slow Road to Safety," *Examiner*, August 6, 2009.

11: Art

For evidence of the Bridge as a signature structure for San Francisco, see *San Francisco*, photographs by Morton Beebe (1989); and *San Francisco,* photographs by Santi Visalli, foreword by Kevin Starr (1990). The poetic response to the Bridge can be seen in Robin Lampson, *The Mending of a Continent* (1937); Joseph Strauss, "The Mighty Task Is Done," in Brown, *Golden Gate*, 229; Elsa Gidlow, *Bridge Builders* (1938); and Stanton A. Coblentz, *From the Golden Gate Bridge* (1947). Regarding Hollywood and the Golden Gate Bridge, see the relevant passages in Jim Van Buskirk and Will Shank, *Celluloid San Francisco: The Film Lover's Guide to Bay Area Movie Locations* (2006). The Web site of the Golden Gate Bridge, Highway, and Transportation District provides a narrative summary and calendar of documents for the seismic retrofit project.

INDEX

INDEX

INDEX

Lawson, Andrew, 68–69, 91, 94, 95, 130
Lawson Report, 91
lawsuits: and financing of the Bridge, 76–77, 82
lead poisoning, 132
L'Enfant, Pierre, 139
Lindenthal, Gustav, 89
Loma Prieta earthquake, 191–92
London, Jack, 22, 59
London, England: bridges in, 11
lumber interests, 64–65
Luttrell, C. J., 66, 67

MacDonald, Alan, 85, 91, 111
MacDonald, Donald, 188, 189, 193
Mackay, Charles, 37
maintenance of Golden Gate Bridge, 190–91, 193–94
Manhattan Bridge (New York City), 88
Marin County
    and BART, 153–54
    Board of Supervisors of, 49, 60
    and calls for building the Bridge, 40–41, 48–49
    and construction of the Bridge, 116, 125
    and development of Bay area, 29–30
    and financing of the Bridge, 75
    GGNRA in, 148
    and opening of the Bridge, 146
    O'Shaughnessy's knowledge of, 48–49
    and politics of building the Bridge, 64, 65, 67
    suburban development in, 49, 155
Marin Headlands, 6, 26, 97, 180
Marin Suicide Prevention Center, 173
Marvelous Marin, 75
Marx, Charles, 78
Massett, Stephen, 37
mathematical analysis: and design of the Bridge, 87, 99–102
Mathews, Arthur, 140–41, 143
Mathews, Lucia, 140–41
Matson Line, 181–82
Maybeck, Bernard, 91
McCoun, W. H., 36
Mediterranean Revival, 142, 143
"The Mending of a Continent" (Lapson), 189–90

Mendocino County, 59, 64, 65–66, 67
Merriam, Frank, 163
Mexican-American War, 32
"The Mighty Task Is Done" (Strauss), 189
minorities, 30, 36, 127, 152
Mission Dolores, 27, 34
missions, Spanish, 26–27, 32, 34, 35
modernism, 13–14
Moisseiff, Leon, 88–89, 91, 95, 96, 98–99, 103, 105, 142, 179
Monterey Bay, 21
Moore, Kermit, 131–32
Morrow, Gertrude Comfort, 93
Morrow, Irving, 91–92, 93–94, 104, 105, 122, 125, 142–43, 178–79, 188–89
Moses, Robert, 89
Motor Car Dealers Association of San Francisco, 62
Moulin, Gabriel, 179
Moulin, Irving, 179
Moulin, Raymond, 179
Mount Hope Bridge (Rhode Island), 117
Mountain Lake, 26
Mouth of the Bay of the Cliffs (La Bocana de la Ensenada de Los Farallones), 24
Mumford, Lewis, 12–13

Napa County, 59, 64, 65, 67, 154
Native Americans, 20–21, 22, 23, 35, 186
Navy, U.S., 4, 31, 107, 145–46, 147
neo-classicism, 139, 141
net
    safety, 133, 135
    steel cable, 173
New Jersey Steel and Iron Co., 48
Neylor, Lewis, 166
North Bay counties
    and benefits of the Bridge, 4, 74, 82
    and calls for building the Bridge, 34
    and financing of the Bridge, 73
    growth and development of, 154–55
    and politics of building the Bridge, 59, 64
    See also specific county
Northwestern Pacific Railroad, 62
Norton, Joshua, 3, 38
Number, 100, 101–2

211

INDEX

A NOTE ON THE AUTHOR

Kevin Starr is university professor and professor of history at the University of Southern California, and state librarian of California emeritus. His seven-part history of California, *Americans and the California Dream*, has earned him the National Medal for the Humanities, the Centennial Medal of the Graduate School of Arts and Sciences of Harvard University, the Gold Medal of the Commonwealth Club of California, a Guggenheim fellowship, and election to the Society of American Historians.